An Educator's Guide to Information Literacy

An Educator's Guide to Information Literacy

What Every High School Senior Needs to Know

Ann Marlow Riedling

LIBRARIES
U N L I M I T E D
A Member of the Greenwood Publishing Group

Westport, Connecticut • London

Library of Congress Cataloging-in-Publication Data

Riedling, Ann Marlow, 1952–

    An educator's guide to information literacy : what every high school senior needs to know / Ann Marlow Riedling.

       p. cm.

    Includes bibliographical references and index.

    ISBN-13: 978-1-59158-446-9 (alk. paper)

    ISBN-10: 1-59158-446-9 (alk. paper)

    1. Information literacy—Study and teaching (Secondary) 2. Information literacy—Standards—United States. 3. Electronic information resource literacy—Study and teaching (Secondary) 4. Research—Methodology—Study and teaching (Secondary) I. Title.

ZA3075.R535 2007

028.7071′2—dc22   2006036844

British Library Cataloguing in Publication Data is available.

Library of Congress Catalog Card Number: 2006036844

ISBN: 978–1–59158–446–9

First published in 2007

Libraries Unlimited, 88 Post Road West, Westport, CT 06881

A Member of the Greenwood Publishing Group, Inc.

www.lu.com

Printed in the United States of America

∞™

The paper used in this book complies with the Permanent Paper Standard issued by the National Information Standards Organization (Z39.48–1984).

10 9 8 7 6 5 4 3 2 1

Contents

1

The Standards: Information Power and ACRL

Conley (2005) conducted a research study called "Standards for Success," which identified the content knowledge in six subject areas that students need in order to succeed in entry level university courses. This study indicates that mastery of not only specific subject content is necessary for success, but also the equally important associated cognitive skills, along with research skills, critical thinking skills, connective intelligence, and the ability to think independently. The study analyzes the limitations of current high school curricula and teaching practices. It presents recommendations to help schools focus on helping students develop necessary knowledge and skills.

Achieve, Inc. (2005) conducted a research project involving recent public high school graduates called "Rising to the Challenge: Are High School Graduates Prepared for College and Work?" In this study, high school graduates (40 percent of whom went on to college and 45 percent went to work) identified research skills as one area in which they were lacking. Details of this study can be found at http://www.achieve.org.

In order to understand the contents of this book, one must first possess a thorough understanding of both sets of information literacy standards: Information Power's and ACRL's. Let's begin with the standards for students in the K–12 environment, *Information Power's Information Literacy Standards for Student Learning*.

Information Power's Information Literacy Standards for Student Learning

As stated in *Information Power* (ALA and AECT 1998), "Information literacy—understanding how to access and use information—is at the core of lifelong learning" (p. vii). First let's take a look at the nine standards:

THE NINE INFORMATION LITERACY STANDARDS FOR STUDENT LEARNING

Information Literacy

Standard 1: The student who is information literate accesses information efficiently and effectively.

Standard 2: The student who is information literate evaluates information critically and competently.

Standard 3: The student who is information literate uses information accurately and creatively.

Independent Learning

Standard 4: The student who is an independent learner is information literate and pursues information related to personal interests.

Standard 5: The student who is an independent learner is information literate and appreciates literature and other creative expressions of information.

Standard 6: The student who is an independent learner is information literate and strives for excellence in information seeking and knowledge generation.

Social Responsibility

Standard 7: The student who contributes positively to the learning community and to society is information literate and recognizes the importance of information to a democratic society.

Standard 8: The student who contributes positively to the learning community and to society is information literate and practices ethical behavior in regard to information and information technology.

Standard 9: The student who contributes positively to the learning community and to society is information literate and participates effectively in groups to pursue and generate information (ALA and AECT 1998, pp. 8, 9).

Now let's take a closer look at each of these standards. The key words in Standard 1 are "accesses information efficiently and effectively." Synonyms of *efficiently* are *resourcefully* and *proficiently*. Students must be organized and know how to locate the precise information they are looking for. They should also know where to look for information—where the best resources are located to meet their particular needs. Students today have access to too much information. Choosing which resource is best to fulfill one's need is complex. With a vast array of online journal indexes, some subject specific and others multidisciplinary, combined with online public access catalogs and dozens of Internet search engines, one can understand why students would opt for the unstructured abundance of information contained in and the simple key-word search approach of the Internet.

The "Indicators" for Standard 1 are:

1. Recognizes the need for information.
2. Recognizes that accurate and comprehensive information is the basis for intelligent decision making.
3. Formulates questions based on information needs.
4. Identifies a variety of potential sources of information.
5. Develops and uses successful strategies for locating information (ALA and AECT 1998, pp. 9–11).

The important message in Standard 2 is "evaluates information critically and competently." This is essential in today's global, technological world. Students still appear to believe that if it is in black-and-white, it is true. They have not been taught the skills to evaluate information for accuracy, bias, appropriateness, scope, relevance, validity, and so forth. Without these skills, the Internet is useless!

The "Indicators" for Standard 2 are:

1. Determines accuracy, relevance, and comprehensiveness.
2. Distinguishes among fact, point of view, and opinion.
3. Identifies inaccurate and misleading information.
4. Selects information appropriate to the problem or question at hand (ALA and AECT 1998, pp. 14, 15).

The important words in Standard 3 are "uses information accurately and creatively." This standard steps forward and "emphasizes the thinking processes involved when students use information to draw conclusions and develop new understandings. ... [students] apply it to decision making, problem solving, critical thinking, and creative expression (ALA and AECT 1998, pp. 18, 19). It is important for us to remember that instruction should be aimed at providing insight into two characteristics of the Internet: the nature of the information it provides and ways to navigate this information.

The "Indicators" for Standard 3 are:

1. Organizes information for practical application.
2. Integrates new information into one's own knowledge.
3. Applies information in critical thinking and problem solving.
4. Produces and communicates information and ideas in appropriate formats (ALA and AECT 1998, pp. 19, 20).

Standard 4 begins the series of independent learning standards. The key words in this standard are "pursues information related to personal interests." A couple of synonyms for *independent* are *self-sufficient* and *autonomous*. Standard 4 is the beginning of students breaking away or conducting effective and efficient research because they have a *personal interest* in a topic. For example, a student may be researching which college or university to attend or what type of car to buy. He or she will use the information literacy skills gained for these personal interests—real world experiences. This is ultimately our goal—to create independent, lifelong learners.

The "Indicators" for Standard 4 are:

1. Seeks information related to various dimensions of personal well-being, such as career interests, community involvement, health matters, and recreational pursuits.
2. Designs, develops, and evaluates information products and solutions related to personal interests (ALA and AECT 1998, p. 23).

The important words in Standard 5 are "appreciates literature and other creative expressions of information." According to *Information Power* "…[Students should] access, evaluate, enjoy, value and create artistic products. That students actively and independently seek to master the principles, conventions, and criteria of literature in print, nonprint, and electronic formats" (ALA and AECT 1998, p. 26).

The "Indicators" for Standard 5 are:

1. Is a competent and self-motivated reader.
2. Derives meaning from information presented creatively in a variety of formats.
3. Develops creative products in a variety of formats (ALA and AECT 1998, pp. 26, 27).

The significant words in Standard 6 are "strives for excellence in information seeking and knowledge generation." Students, in spite of their technological genius, are not experienced researchers. While seemingly rewarded by the number of hits they receive, students often get frustrated and end up resorting to surfing from one site to another in hopes of discovering that one gold nugget of information. Sometimes students abandon their search completely and claim they could not find anything on their topic. Therefore, instruction again should be aimed at giving insight into two areas of the Internet: the nature of the information it provides and ways to navigate this information.

The "Indicators" for Standard 6 are:

1. Assesses the quality of the process and products of personal information seeking.
2. Devises strategies for revising, improving, and updating self-generated knowledge (ALA and AECT 1998, pp. 29, 30).

Standard 7 begins the area of social responsibility standards. The key words in Standard 7 are "recognizes the importance of information to a democratic society." According to *Information Power* (ALA and AECT 1998), students should seek out information from a diversity of viewpoints, scholarly traditions, and cultural perspectives in an attempt to arrive at a reasoned and informed understanding of issues. They should realize that equitable access to information from a range of sources and in all formats is a fundamental right in a democracy.

The "Indicators" for Standard 7 are:

1. Seeks information from diverse sources, contexts, disciplines, and cultures.
2. Respects the principle of equitable access to information (ALA and AECT 1998, p. 33).

The vital words in Standard 8 are "practices ethical behavior in regard to information and information technology." We are honored to live in a democratic society. We must share this over and over again with our students, along with the principles of intellectual freedom and the rights of producers of intellectual property. What is ethical? It is moral, decent, and just.

The "Indicators" for Standard 8 are:

1. Respects the principles of intellectual freedom.
2. Respects intellectual property rights.
3. Uses information technology responsibly (ALA and AECT 1998, pp. 36, 37).

The key words in Standard 9 are "participates effectively in groups to pursue and generate information." This standard speaks of collaborating with diverse groups and cultures to locate information or seek solutions.

The "Indicators" for Standard 9 are:

1. Shares knowledge and information with others.
2. Respects others' ideas and backgrounds and acknowledges their contributions.
3. Collaborates with others, both in person and through technologies, to identify information problems and to seek their solutions.
4. Collaborates with others, both in person and through technologies, to design, develop, and evaluate information products and solutions (ALA and AECT 1998, pp. 39–41).

Students must master information literacy skills if they are to harness the potential of this new age of information. By working together, we can prepare students with the necessary skills for college and life to ensure that this new millennium is not remembered as the age of *mis*information.

Information Literacy Competency Standards for Higher Education

The Association of College and Research Libraries (ACRL) *Information Literacy Competency Standards for Higher Education* were approved by the American Library Association (ALA) in 2000 and endorsed by the American Association of Higher Education (AAHE). According to ACRL, information literacy is a set of abilities requiring individuals to recognize when information is needed and have the ability to locate, evaluate, and effectively use the needed information. In addition, information literacy forms the basis for lifelong learning; it is common to all disciplines, to all learning environments, and to all levels of education. It enables learners to master content and extend their research, become more self-directed, and gain greater control over their own learning.

An information literate individual is able to:

- Determine the extent of information needed
- Access the needed information effectively and efficiently
- Evaluate information and its sources critically
- Incorporate selected information into his or her knowledge base
- Use information effectively to accomplish a specific purpose
- Understand the economic, legal, and social issues surrounding the use of information, and access and use information ethically and legally

---

The amount and complexity of information with which students have to deal is growing by leaps and bounds. As a result, no course of study, especially in higher education, is adequate unless it helps to develop students' ability to deal with the rapidly increasing information in their fields.

ACRL believes that developing lifelong learners is central to the mission of higher education institutions. By ensuring that students have the intellectual abilities of reasoning and critical thinking, and by helping them construct a framework for learning how to learn, colleges and universities provide the foundation for continued growth throughout their careers, as well as in their roles as informed citizens and members of communities.

According to Quarton (2003), the abilities to explore information resources efficiently and to critically evaluate the results are basic information skills. They are best developed through regular exposure to assignments that are process oriented and that require critical thinking. Students who know how to use information resources and who recognize the essential characteristics and purposes of published materials have a critical advantage when adding to their knowledge base in any discipline; they also have a firm foundation for future course work. Further, because information literacy skills are transferable to other disciplines and to everyday life, students' future learning—both in and out of the classroom—is positively impacted.

Information Literacy Competency Standards for Higher Education provides a framework for assessing the information literate student. It also extends the work of the American Association of School Librarians (AASL) Task Force on Information Literacy Standards, thereby providing higher education an opportunity to articulate its information literacy competencies with those of K–12 so that a continuum of expectations develops for students at all levels. Students will also find the competencies useful because they provide a framework for gaining control over interactions with information in their environment.

Information Literacy Competency Standards for Higher Education consists of 5 standards, 22 performance indicators, and a wide range of outcomes for assessing student progress toward information literacy.

Information Literacy Competency Standards for Student Learning

Standard 1: The information literate student determines the nature and extent of the information needed.

Standard 2: The information literate student accesses needed information effectively and efficiently.

Standard 3: The information literate student evaluates information and its sources critically and incorporates selected information into his or her knowledge base and value system.

Standard 4: The information literate student, individually or as a member of a group, uses information effectively to accomplish a specific purpose.

Standard 5: The information literate student understands many of the ethical, legal, and socio-economic issues surrounding the use of information and accesses and uses information ethically and legally (ACRL 2000, p. x).

Now let's take a closer look at each of these standards. The critical words in Standard 1 are "determines the nature and extent of the information needed." To accomplish this standard, students should confer with various people and resources to identify a research topic and/or increase familiarity with the topic. In addition, students should develop a thesis statement, formulate questions based on the information need, and modify this need to achieve a manageable focus. Students must also identify concepts and terms that describe the information need and recognize that existing information can be combined with original thought to produce new information. Within this standard, we see that students should identify the value and differences of potential resources in a variety of formats, as well as differentiate between primary and secondary sources. Finally, students should define a realistic overall plan and timeline to acquire the needed information and review the information need to clarify, revise, or refine the question.

The "Performance Indicators" for Standard 1 are:

1. The information literate student defines and articulates the need for information.
2. The information literate student identifies a variety of types and formats of potential sources for information.
3. The information literate student considers the costs and benefits of acquiring the needed information.
4. The information literate student reevaluates the nature and extent of the information need (ACRL 2000, p. x).

The key words in Standard 2 are "accesses needed information effectively and efficiently." To accomplish Standard 2, students should identify appropriate investigative methods, as well as the scope, content, and organization of information retrieval systems. It is also important that students develop a research plan appropriate to the investigative method and are able to construct a search strategy using appropriate commands for the information retrieval system selected. Students should also use various search systems to retrieve information in a variety of formats and use various classification schemes and other systems to locate information resources. Finally, students must assess the quantity, quality, and relevance of the search and identify gaps in the information retrieved.

The "Performance Indicators" for Standard 2 are:

1. The information literate student selects the most appropriate investigative methods or information retrieval systems for accessing the needed information.
2. The information literate student constructs and implements effectively designed search strategies.
3. The information literate student retrieves information online or in person using a variety of methods.
4. The information literate student refines the search strategy if necessary.
5. The information literate student extracts, records, and manages the information and its sources (ACRL 2000, p. x).

Standard 3's key words are "evaluates information and its sources critically and incorporates selected information into his or her knowledge base and value system." In order to accomplish this, students must be able to paraphrase or summarize information after reading a wide variety of resources and selecting main ideas. In addition, it is vital that students examine and compare information from various sources to evaluate reliability, validity, accuracy, authority, timeliness, and point of view or bias. Students should also recognize interrelationships among concepts. They must also draw conclusions based on information gathered, investigate differing viewpoints, seek expert opinions, and determine if the original information need has been satisfied or if more information is required.

The "Performance Indicators" for Standard 3 are:

1. The information literate student summarizes the main ideas to be extracted from the information gathered.
2. The information literate student articulates and applies initial criteria for evaluating both the information and its sources.
3. The information literate student synthesizes main ideas to construct new concepts.

> 4. The information literate student compares new knowledge with prior knowledge to determine the value added, contradictions, or other unique characteristics of the information.
> 5. The information literate student determines whether the new knowledge has an impact on the individual's value system and takes steps to reconcile differences.
> 6. The information literate student validates understanding and interpretation of the information through discourse with other individuals, subject-area experts, and/or practitioners.
> 7. The information literate student determines whether the initial query should be revised (ACRL 2000, p. x).

Standard 4's important words are "uses information effectively to accomplish a specific purpose." To meet Standard 4, students must organize the content, articulate knowledge and skills from previous experiences, integrate the new and prior information, and manipulate digital text, images, and so forth. Additionally, students should reflect on past successes, failures, and alternative strategies. They must also choose a communication medium or format that supports the purposes of the product and the intended audience, incorporate principles of design and communication, and clearly communicate with a style that supports the purposes of the intended audience.

> **The "Performance Indicators" for Standard 4 are:**
>
> 1. The information literate student, individually or as a member of a group, uses information effectively to accomplish a specific purpose.
> 2. The information literate student revises the development for the product or performance.
> 3. The information literate student communicates the product or performance effectively to others (ACRL 2000, p. x).

The key words in Standard 5 are "understands many of the ethical, legal, and socio-economic issues surrounding the use of information and accesses and uses information ethically and legally." To accomplish this standard, students must identify and discuss issues related to privacy and security, free and fee-based access to information, and censorship and freedom of speech. They should also demonstrate an understanding of intellectual property, copyright, and fair use of copyrighted material. In addition, students must legally obtain, store, and disseminate text, data, images, or sounds and demonstrate an understanding of what constitutes plagiarism. Finally, they should select an appropriate documentation style and post permission-granted notices, as needed, for copyrighted material.

The "Performance Indicators" for Standard 5 are:

1. The information literate student understands many of the ethical, legal, and socio-economic issues surrounding information and information technology.
2. The information literate student follows laws, regulations, institutional policies, and etiquette related to the access and use of information resources.
3. The information literate student acknowledges the use of information sources in communicating the product or performance (ACRL 2000, p. x).

It is critical for us to remind students that the sheer abundance of information will not in itself create a more informed citizenry—not without a complementary cluster of abilities necessary to use information effectively. The uncertain quality and expanding quantity of information pose large challenges for our society today. It is our responsibility to use these tools to teach our youth the information literacy skills necessary to thrive in the world in which they, and the generations after them, will live.

2

Information Literacy: A Review of the Literature

One thing is certain—there is no lack of information regarding information literacy! Numerous books, articles, and studies have been written about this "hot" topic of the twenty-first century. In order to better understand its importance, we should have a broad working knowledge of information literacy from a wide variety of angles.

"College librarians and high school library media specialists have lots to share with one another...college librarians and high school media specialists face many similar issues and challenges, and the solutions we find adapt from one level to another" (Donham 2003, p. 1). That being said, a study was conducted by Diane Mittermeyer that looked at the following question: "When entering the first year of undergraduate study, how information literate are the students? Over 3,000 participants returned a mail questionnaire representing a response rate of 56%...the results indicated that for many respondents, their knowledge of the basic elements characterizing the information seeking process is rather limited" (Mittermeyer 2005, p. 203). Mittermeyer goes on to explain that academic librarians are still very concerned by what seems to be a low level of knowledge regarding the information-seeking process, particularly among incoming first-year undergraduate students. While profound changes have marked the ways librarians have defined and implemented information literacy programs since the early 1990s, the interest in this aspect of university education has significantly increased in recent years. The publication of the ACRL *Information Literacy Competency Standards for Higher Education* in 2000 constituted an important event. The development and publication of these standards highlighted the importance and role of education in the use of information, not only in academic pursuits, but also in the broader context of lifelong learning.

The concept of information literacy is not recent; in fact, it dates back to at least 1986 (Doyle 1995). By 1994, Bleakley and Carrigan were able to state definitively that due to our overly rich information environment, information literacy had become a new basic skill. They concluded that in order to develop information literate students, library media specialists and classroom teachers must assume new roles. The term *information literacy* has been in use for almost 20 years internationally. In 1995, Carol Kulthau noted three important trends in library media center instruction, the first being a shift from instruction in library skills to instruction in information skills and information literacy. Kulthau also predicted a shift to process orientation in skills instruction and increased integration of information skills into the curriculum. In 2000, Moore conducted a study that indicated that the majority of teachers did not have a clear understanding of the concept of information literacy and tended to confuse it with research or library skills. Even more recently, Whelan (2003) conducted a survey involving more than 800 school librarians on information literacy and their instructional role. The results indicated that neither teachers nor students recognized the importance of skills tied to information literacy. Whelan also indicated that the main barrier to implementing information literacy is a lack of support from classroom teachers, many of whom don't really know what information literacy is. Katherine Miller conducted a study of pre-service teachers in 2003 regarding librarians and information literacy. The results indicated that most participants had positive recollections of librarians from their high school and university days. However, when asked "how their pre-service training prepared them to work with school librarians, the teachers were unanimous in their responses—"not at all." When asked about their understanding of information literacy, all of the pre-service teachers agreed that they had never heard the term information literacy. Because these teachers were unfamiliar with this term, none of them felt they had been specifically prepared to implement it in their classrooms. However, all pre-service teachers agreed that the school librarian could help them in meeting instructional goals. After completing the study, Miller provided three recommendations: 1) practicing school librarians need to get involved with teacher training programs, 2) school librarians should mentor new teachers and staff members, and 3) school librarians need to become advocates for information literacy. Despite these studies, it is apparent that some high schools and teacher-training institutions are not preparing students and prospective teachers to understand the concept of and need for instruction in information literacy. The concept of information literacy should be known and understood by librarians, administrators, and students, and the term information literacy should be a part of the current vocabulary of every stakeholder in every school and institution.

Mackey and Jacobson (2004) state that information literacy is an essential skills set that prepares students for critical thinking in college, the workplace, and everyday life. Students who are information literate are better equipped for today's multifaceted information environment than those students who are not. Though some campuses place a greater focus on information literacy instruction than others, most are struggling to find ways to include information literacy programs at the undergraduate level. Mackey and Jacobson go on to explain that information literacy prepares students for college research, but also introduces a way of thinking about information that is device-independent. That is, information literacy focuses on the analytical evaluation and production of information in a variety of forms regardless of changing technology. Information literate students pursue knowledge and understanding through research, writing, and communication while advancing these activities through ongoing practice. "This integrated approach to information literacy informs three proposed teaching models: 1) The Art of Annotation: Teaching students to conduct research in the library and online to synthesize and document information for the development of annotated bibliography, 2) Research and Composition: Teaching students to incorporate discipline-specific resources (i.e., scholarly journal articles and professional Web sites) in properly documented research essays, and 3) Writing for the Web: Teaching students to develop content for the Internet with a specific focus on primary and secondary research methods" (Mackey and Jacobson 2004, p. 202).

According to Breivik (1998), "the best place to start information literacy planning is with general education or core curriculum, where concerns for competencies that all students should acquire provide a natural home for the discussion of information literacy abilities" (p. 44). She argues for "resource-based learning" in which students access, evaluate, organize, and present information from all the real-world sources existing in today's information society. Sellen (2002) argues for an active-learning approach to information literacy in general education. She states "information literacy brings to general education the acquisition of new learning skills and takes advantage of technological advancements of the 21st century" (p. 116). Lou and MacGregor (2004) remark that resource-based learning has great potential to improve the development of higher-order cognitive skills, critical thinking, and problem solving skills that the fast-paced information age demands. According to Rockman (2002), information literacy must be available to "first year, lower-division, transfer, upper-division, senior and graduate students" (p. 195). However, it must also be linked to an ongoing assessment process that will provide meaningful feedback to instructors and the institution about the quality of these initiatives and the impact this work has on student learning.

According to Boekhorst and Britz (2004), information literacy has become one of the most important skills in the information society and governments have a specific responsibility to their citizens to prepare them for the challenges posed by the era in which Dumont and Fenoulhet (1977) are living. They contend that: 1) information and knowledge have become the most important assets of society, 2) the primary economic questions no longer deal with scarcity, but focus on the management of the abundance of information that has become available as a result of technology (Dumont and Fenoulhet 1977), and 3) the rapid development of information and communication technologies has become the engine in the process of globalization. They go on to explain that to be able to function adequately in a society that is oriented towards information, people need to become more information literate than ever before. These skills are only partly learned in daily life; they should also be a major portion of the school curriculum.

Heil (2005) states "to use the Internet effectively, students need to be taught critical evaluation skills that they can apply to each web site they use for research" (p. 26). She goes on to explain that Internet users have developed an infatuation with information, and the more of it the better, as long as it is easy to obtain. Haycock (2006) states that students usually choose less reliable commercial sites over educational or government sites for their research even though only approximately one fourth of the commercial sites are suitable for academic purposes.

Breivik (2005) explains that education has always had the responsibility to help students acquire research skills. She also states that despite the growing recognition that today's students must be information literate, higher education is just beginning to define what it means to be so. Breivik states, "It is a world with an over abundance, indeed, a tidal-wave of information that bombards them from the time they turn on the television in the morning to the moment they turn off the computer before they go to sleep. In between, they gather information from messages on cell phones, books, magazines, DVDs and a multitude of other sources. Young people today send and receive emails, engage in chat rooms, and find most of the information they use on the Internet" (2005, p. 2). Breivik also remarks that students' major attraction to search engines like Google is that they save time, and despite the interest of some accreditors and the evidence of the need for information literacy skills in the workplace, few campuses have systematically addressed this need. "It is time for both technology and information literacy skills to be accepted as a core competency to be acquired systematically through all levels of formal learning. The effort to develop them should begin in the K–12 system. . . . But all of these efforts will not accomplish anything if classroom faculty are not committed to developing the information literacy skills of their students. Not many faculties seem to have that commitment. Some operate on the comfortable assumption that students acquire these skills before coming to their classes. Efforts to develop students' information literacy skills in college need to take place at the institutional, program and classroom levels" (Breivik 2005, p. 24).

As explained by Rosen and Castro (2002), "Thousands of new students arrive at information-rich academic libraries every fall, thirsting for knowledge but not bringing a cup. . . . The term 'information literacy' is on everyone's lips in college and university libraries these days. But how do you take those thousands of fresh, new faces and help them to understand when they need information, where to look, and how to evaluate what they find—in short, how do you teach them to become information literate?" (p. 30). Caroline Geck (2006) states that according to the Encarta World English Dictionary, Generation Y is defined as people born in or after 1980. Although Generation Z is not yet defined in the dictionary, the term is sometimes used to describe the already existing net generation of teenagers born in or after 1990 in technologically advanced countries. Today's Generation Z is currently comprised of 1-year-olds or those approaching their early teens; these youths were born into a totally different technological world than their immediate predecessors (Generation Y) were. In fact, the Generation Z birth years closely correspond to the conception and birth of the World Wide Web. However, even though these youths had early experiences with digital technologies, they do not have a deep understanding of the inner workings of the Internet or how commercial search engines rank results. Many of these students have never engaged in formal exercises comparing advantages, disadvantages, strengths, and weaknesses of the Web with other information tools such as books and print journals. Members of other generations are more likely to do this sort of mental comparison automatically. Teenagers' inabilities to use the Web effectively and efficiently cause them to spend exorbitant amounts of time browsing. These students often started using the Internet before having been given any sort of formal instruction about locating and evaluating Web pages. This group's preferred method of Internet searching is to start with a Google search, even if that may not be the most efficient or fastest means to the answer. This suggests that these teens are not information literate.

According to Scott and O'Sullivan (2005), "High school students, in spite of their bravura, are not experienced Internet researchers. High school students frequently have difficulty defining exactly what kind of information they need" (p. 21). As the Internet redefines what we determine to be knowledge, it creates a cognitive divide between those who can effectively navigate and negotiate the information domains of hypertext and hypermedia (the information rich) and those who cannot (the information poor) (Scott and O'Sullivan 2005). As McPhearson (2005) explains, surfing the Internet is more challenging than finding information about needles in a set of Dorling Kindersley's Eyewitness Books series! If only the Internet came with a good table of contents or an index! Although the feasibility of an Internet index can be debated, most Web page designers will not argue the necessity for clearly organizing Web site content.

According to Mackey and Jacobson (2005) at the University at Albany, State University of New York, collaboration among faculty and librarians is essential for information literacy initiatives to be successful. Faculty and librarians work together on program planning, course development, course approval, and teaching. This collaborative experience was positive and demonstrated that a similar model would benefit other institutions considering information literacy initiatives. Librarians work with students on their research assignments, and are well informed about students' research skills and the resources available to them to complete their assignments. With the lines of communication open, faculty can provide input to librarians about student experiences with library resources and offer useful suggestions for research materials, information organization, technology access, databases, and so forth. In 1999, the University at Albany established an information literacy subcommittee. It was responsible for developing the characteristics that all information literacy courses at the university must meet. This subcommittee reviews proposals for potential information literacy courses; develops assessment criteria for students taking these courses; and brainstorms ways to make sure that there are sufficient options for students who need to meet their general education requirement. As a result, information literacy at this institution of higher education has been advanced through collaboration among faculty and librarians. In today's information environment, students must be prepared for a level of inquiry that extends beyond the fixed space and time of a single class, semester or location. It is imperative to conceptualize scalable information literacy teaching models and realistically demonstrate the benefits for the students. The entire process allows them to be more prepared for successful assessment and self-study. Librarians and faculty are in a unique position to facilitate the collaborative information literacy endeavor in the classroom, library, online, and on campus.

As stated by Rockman and Smith (2005), research has shown that in order to develop information literacy skills, students must be given repeated opportunities to acquire and exercise these skills in their daily lives. Breivik (2005) states that the new challenge faced by educators today is created by the very environment in which today's children live and learn. It is a world of overabundance that bombards them from the time they turn on the television in the morning to the moment they turn off the computer at night. Without a doubt, these young people are far more awash in information than their parents were. However, neither all of this information, nor their ease with computers and the Internet are translating into better-educated and informed students or workers. Breivik goes on to explain, "Nowhere is the need for information literacy skills greater than in today's work environment, where efforts to manage knowledge are increasingly necessary to keep a strategic advantage within a global market. The list of business leaders calling for information literate workers keeps growing" (2005, p. 21).

Peter Drucker, the eminent management scholar, was an early proponent of information literacy. In a 1992 *Wall Street Journal* article, he warned, "Few executives yet know how to ask: 'What information do I need to do my job? When do I need it? In what form? And from whom should I be getting it?" (p. 3). The continuing concern with information overload and the inability of most people to deal with it are indications of the low level of understanding of information management within organizations. To achieve this, information literacy skills much be actively and visibly valued by the organization and people must be given the time, space, and encouragement to develop them.

As explained by Todd (2001), studies show that when using the Internet, students: 1) prefer browsing to systematic search strategies, 2) examine only the first screen of most sites, 3) perform only two or three inquiries per search, 4) make quick decisions, 5) construct an answer on limited information, 6) are satisfied with somewhat-relevant hit, and 7) have a tendency to plagiarize. In a study conducted by Hoctor (2005), in a remote area of the United States, it was discovered that teenagers would choose a cell phone and computer as opposed to other practical items. Most adults considered these electronic devices a luxury; most youths saw them as a necessity. As digital immigrants we must assume the responsibility of ensuring that students are prepared to be effective and productive and have the tools, vocabulary, and skills to function as lifelong learners, participant, and contributors in the twenty-first century (Dorsaj and Jukes 2004). Davis (2004) explained that she felt it was time to push for formalized information and technology literacy programs. As a result, the following occurred: 1) more exploratory writing assignments occurred, 2) teachers wanted to talk about information literacy and appreciated the collaborative effort by the school librarian, 3) online databases were extremely useful and should be promoted, and 4) teachers recognized that the Internet has major—and a variety of—shortcomings.

In a study conducted by Hensley (2004), it was discovered that the first step in solving the problem of putting curiosity and creativity back into pedagogy is achieving a better understanding of what they are. According to Evans and Harrar (2002), curious people have five attributes: 1) nudge conversation with new ideas, 2) take pleasure in learning about other people and show it, 3) focus on the person they are with, 4) use jokes and humor to liven things up, and 5) accentuate the positive about what they like about their conversational partner or the conversation itself. Upon further investigation it was determined that an environment that promotes curiosity in isolation does not promote learning or create new knowledge. Creativity must also be encouraged for learning to occur successfully. Hensley goes on to explain that, "If information literacy experts believe that curiosity and creativity are the attributes that characterize the inquiring intellect, that as professional educators we must accept the premise that learning is more about the individual than the masses. Successful teaching and learning encounters have one element in common: At the heart of these is a curious and creative individual, student, or library user who can sustain ongoing appreciation for what learning is and how information promotes and nurtures, developing awareness, ability, self-confidence, and contribution" (Hensley, p. 32). To accomplish these, we must change our perspectives regarding what we teach and how we teach it. Information literacy is the base for it all.

As explained by Gratch-Lindauer (2004), traditional measures of information literacy assessment focus primarily on student learning outcomes, but student learning outcomes are not the only important area of assessment. It is equally important to measure and document personal experiences that directly contribute to the development of information literate individuals, such as specific indicators that capture the quality of the learning environment and learner self-assessment of skills and instruction/learning satisfaction ratings. She explains that a large part of assessing information literacy deals with performance-based approaches. She purports that it is imperative that librarians undertake information literacy assessment projects regularly.

Peter Levine (2005) remarks that false information is not a recent phenomenon. No individual knows enough about any field to make judgments about the truth or falsehood of every claim within that field. It is the responsibility of schools/institutions of higher education to improve information literacy in all respects. However, Levine also explains that students are already using the World Wide Web to do standard kinds of assigned research, so they must be taught how to identify reliable sites if they are going to do good work in their courses. That being stated, schools must teach students to identify reliable and unreliable information. This task in quite demanding. Levine explains that effective instruction in information literacy involves emotions and attitudes, not just skills and knowledge. A student who is afraid of computers, discouraged by the complexity of a topic, bored of the content being studied, or cynical about all information courses cannot learn to distinguish reliable from unreliable online information. The need to change attitudes as well as knowledge and skills is difficult. Levine promotes actively providing reliable sources of online information. Finally, she explains that if there were prominent and reliable portals in each important field, then everyone would have the relatively simple job of saying "yes!"

Stanley Wilder (2005) states that information literacy is the wrong solution to the wrong problem facing librarianship. It mistakes the nature of the Internet threat and it offers a response at odds with higher education's traditional mission. This article explains that librarians should not assume that college students welcome their help in doing online research. He goes on to explain that only librarians like to search; everyone else likes to find. Although this is not a positive reaction to information literacy, it should be noted.

As stated by Ishizuka (2005), Internet users are far too cocky about their online search abilities, but in reality, most don't know the origin or validity of the content they find. Many people are under the impression that everything on the Internet is of equal value. They also expect that the most relevant and accurate information will appear at the top of the browser window when they search. If students understood how browsers work, they would be in a better position to select specific browsers for specific tasks. Another key element of teaching students to be information literate is to stress using online databases and other tools (i.e., subject directories) that have been "selected as fact."

As Jenson (2004) explains, much of the research that students now do is conducted online; the context of that research has been lost. In addition, she remarks that professors complain about the quality of their students' end products, while at the same time students express equal frustration that they can't find anything on the topics addressed. Jenson goes on to state that students have trouble producing good research because they have not been given the foundation necessary for doing so in a world where research of the available literature is now conducted almost exclusively by looking at a computer monitor. In fact, students can be taught effective research skills despite the complexity of the electronic indexes and databases now used for research. What is the crux of the problem? Students lack hands-on experience in an actual library and with actual library materials, the type of experience that the vast majority of us in the teaching sector rely on.

According to Abilock (2004), "…students recognize that information literacy is not a school task but a lifetime habit of mind—of evaluating and using information for personal, social, or global purposes….Information literacy is a transformational process in which the learner needs to find, understand, evaluate and use information in various forms to create for personal, social or global purposes…when I have been successful at designing and creating an environment in which the questions asked are genuine, my students have given me permission—indeed invited me—to teach rigorous thinking. And, when I am presented with the gift of a student's intuition I am the learner, too, asking rather than answering" (p. 10).

3

Lessons for Each ACRL Standard

Lessons for Standard 1

Standard 1 is as follows: The information literate student determines the nature and extent of the information needed.

Performance Indicators: The information literate student defines and articulates the need for information.

Outcomes include:

- Confers with instructors and participates in class discussions, peer workgroups, and electronic discussions to identify a research topic, or other information need
- Develops a thesis statement and formulates questions based on the information need
- Explores general information sources to increase familiarity with the topic
- Defines and modifies the information need to achieve a manageable focus
- Identifies key concepts and terms that describe the information need
- Recognizes that existing information can be combined with original thought, experimentation, and/or analysis to produce new information

The information literate student identifies a variety of types and formats of potential sources for information.

Outcomes include:

- Knows how information is formally and informally produced, organized, and disseminated
- Recognizes that knowledge can be organized into disciplines that influence the way information is accessed
- Identifies the purpose and audience of potential resources (e.g., popular vs. scholarly, current vs. historical)
- Differentiates between primary and secondary sources, recognizing how their use and importance vary with each discipline
- Realizes that information may need to be constructed with raw data from primary sources

The information literate student considers the costs and benefits of acquiring the needed information.

Outcomes include:

- Determines the availability of needed information and makes decisions on broadening the information seeking process beyond local resources (e.g., interlibrary loan; using resources at other locations; obtaining images, videos, text, or sound)
- Considers the feasibility of acquiring a new language or skill (e.g., foreign or discipline-based) in order to gather needed information and to understand its context

The information literate student reevaluates the nature and extent of the information need.

Outcomes include:

- Reviews the initial information need to clarify, revise, or refine the question
- Describes criteria used to make information decisions and choices

Lesson 3.1: Choosing a Topic

NAME: _____ DATE: _____

What are you going to research? Sometimes, choosing a topic is the most difficult part of conducting research. Your instructor may assign you a topic or the choice may be yours. Knowing where to locate ideas will help you find an interesting, exciting research topic.

So, where can you get ideas? There are a number of places to look. Sometimes, just focusing on your specific interests, the things you have read about and conversations with others is a good place to start. Otherwise, current journals and magazines can be used to locate timely research topics. Also, browsing the shelves of a library may spur an interesting topic. Encyclopedias (and subject encyclopedias) are good sources for topics. Finally, the Internet can be an extremely useful place to locate ideas. Several good Web sites for obtaining research topics are:

http://lib1.uwec.edu/research/index.asp
http://library.sau.edu/bestinfo/Hot/hotindex.htm
http://poynteronline.org/column.asp?id=49
http://www.nwmissouri.edu/library/courses/english2/termindex.htm

Using one or more of the resources listed above, choose a research topic of interest to you. Remember to keep the following in mind:

- It should not be too broad or too narrow.
- It should keep your interest for a period of time.
- It should be a topic for which you can locate information easily.

Also, by answering the following questions, your research will become more organized:

- What kind of assignment is it? (e.g., is it a 50-page paper, a 3-minute oral presentation, or a PowerPoint presentation?)
- Will you be able to find enough information about your topic—how much information do you need?
- What kind of information do you need? (e.g., statistical, opinion, etc.)
- Is currency of information important?
- What formats do you need? (e.g., printed, electronic, visual, audio, etc.)
- How much time do you have?

For this lesson, research as explained above and determine a topic of interest to you

YOUR TOPIC: _____

HOW DID YOU ARRIVE AT THIS TOPIC?

Lesson 3.2: Question Brainstormer

	Topic #1	Topic #2
Which one? (Collect information to make an informed choice.) (e.g., Which twentieth century president did the most to promote civil rights?)		
How? (Understand problems and perspectives, weigh options, and propose solutions.) (e.g., How should we solve the problem of water pollution in our neighborhood?)		
What if? (Use the knowledge you have to pose a hypothesis and consider options.) (e.g., What if the Declaration of Independence abolished slavery?)		
Should? (Make a moral or practical decision based on evidence.) (e.g., Should we clone humans?)		
Why? (Understand and explain relationships to get to the essence of a complicated issue.) (e.g., Why do people abuse children?)		

Permission granted by Joyce Valenza, 2006.

Brainstorm two topics related to the unit we are studying. Use the cues to develop essential questions that will help you focus your research. You don't need to fill in every box. We will be discussing which of the questions you develop would be the best to research.

From *An Educator's Guide to Information Literacy: What Every High School Senior Needs to Know*. Westport, CT: Libraries Unlimited, 2007. Copyright © 2007 by Ann Marlow Riedling.

Lesson 3.3: Developing Your Question

NAME: _____ DATE: _____

Once you have identified your topic, think about questions your research might help you answer. In other words, state your topic as a question. Think about significant key words that describe your topic. The key words you choose will become essential for searching catalogs, indexes, Web sites, and databases regarding information about your topic.

Now do the following concerning your research topic:

YOUR TOPIC: _____

1. Write what you THINK you know about your topic.

2. Develop five or more questions about your topic (The following may help you with this: Why? How? Which one? What if? Should? Why?)

3. List 10 keywords regarding your topic.

Remember, your research question may change as you learn more about your topic. This is perfectly fine!

From *An Educator's Guide to Information Literacy: What Every High School Senior Needs to Know.* Westport, CT: Libraries Unlimited, 2007. Copyright © 2007 by Ann Marlow Riedling.

Lesson 3.4: Narrowing/Refining a Topic

NAME: _____ DATE: _____

Once you have found some background information about your topic, you can refine it to a more narrow, focused topic. It is critical that your research topic not be too broad or too narrow. For a research topic that is too broad, it will be difficult to limit the amount you write and the topic will not be adequately covered. For a topic that is too narrow, it is difficult to locate enough useful information to write about it adequately.

Answer the following question before narrowing your topic to a manageable size:

1. What do I already know about the topic?
2. Do I want to cover a specific time period?
3. Is there a geographic location on which I want to focus?
4. Is there a particular aspect of the topic that interests me?

Try narrowing your topic by using the following:

- Time
- Location
- Genre or event
- Area of study

For example, let's say the topic you chose is "music." Obviously, that is much too broad of a topic. If you narrowed it with regard to time, it might be the 1960s. Now, if you narrow it further by location, it could be the United States. Narrowing it by genre might be Rock and Roll; finally, narrowing it by area of study could be the influence of the Beatles on Rock and Roll.

Now you try this with your topic:

TOPIC: _____

Time: _____

Location: _____

Genre: _____

Area of Study: _____

FINAL REVISED TOPIC: _____

From *An Educator's Guide to Information Literacy: What Every High School Senior Needs to Know*. Westport, CT: Libraries Unlimited, 2007. Copyright © 2007 by Ann Marlow Riedling.

Lesson 3.5: Selecting Appropriate Sources of Information

NAME: _____ DATE: _____

It is vitally important to select appropriate resources for your research topic. For example, if your topic deals with dinosaurs, the Internet may not be the most useful place to look; reference and other books would be helpful. Likewise, if your topic concerns the current presidential elections, the Internet and recent periodicals may be the best places to look because your topic requires current information.

For this lesson, locate at least one specific resource in each of the following categories that is pertinent to your topic. However, if a particular source would not have information about your topic, leave it blank and explain why it would not include useful information. The following may be helpful regarding types of reference books.

Types of Reference Books

Dictionaries and encyclopedias are some of the most common types of reference works, but there are many kinds. The following is a list of reference books, what they do, and an example for each:

- **Dictionaries and Thesauri**—give word meanings, spellings, and histories (dictionaries) or synonyms and related words (thesaurus).
  Example: *Merriam-Webster's Collegiate Dictionary*
- **Encyclopedias**—contain articles on subjects in various fields, usually including helpful bibliographies. They can be either general or specialized.
  General example: *World Book Encyclopedia*
  Specialized example: *Man, Myth and Magic*
- **Indexes**—tell where information can be found in other sources.
  Example: Poetry Index
- **Yearbooks**—often called annuals, chronicle the events of a certain year, usually in a particular field.
  Example: Current Biography
- **Handbooks and Manuals**—are often "how to" books, containing instructions and miscellaneous items of information on one subject.
  Example: *Occupational Outlook Handbook*
- **Almanacs**—are collections of facts, charts, and statistics.
  Example: *World Almanac and Book of Facts*
- **Biographical Sources**—provide short sketches about the lives of important people.
  Example: *Encyclopedia of World Biography*
- **Directories**—list names and addresses of persons, organizations, and businesses.
  Example: a telephone book

From *An Educator's Guide to Information Literacy: What Every High School Senior Needs to Know*. Westport, CT: Libraries Unlimited, 2007. Copyright © 2007 by Ann Marlow Riedling.

- **Atlases and Gazetteers**—are visual representations (atlases) or geographical dictionaries (gazetteers) that provide information about places.
  Example: *Book of the World*
- **Statistical Sources**—give data or numbers that have been compiled to quantify and compare the characteristics of people, places or things
  Example: *Statistical Abstract of the United States*

TOPIC: _____

- Book
- Magazine
- Scholarly journal
- Newspaper
- Pamphlet
- Reference material (encyclopedia, dictionary, thesauri, yearbook, handbook, manual, almanac, biographical source, directory, atlas, statistical resource)
- Video or DVD
- Sound recording
- Interview
- Online database encyclopedia
- Online database book
- Online database journal article
- Online database newspaper article
- e-Book
- Internet
- E-mail
- Listserv

Lesson 3.6: Background Information

NAME: _____ DATE: _____

In order to begin your research, you need to know important facts related to your research, including:

- Names of key people
- Dates
- History or development of the topic
- Important events

- Key words
- Definitions
- Current issues
- Any other useful facts

Resources:

Type of Research	Background information sources
Historic topics	General encyclopedias, specialized encyclopedias, biographical dictionaries, other reference books
Recent events or topics	Periodical and newspaper articles, online databases, reliable Internet sites

Research Topic: _____

Information Source Used:

Author(s)/Editor(s)_____

Title _____

_____ Reference Book _____ Periodical/Journal Article _____ Internet Site

1. Record key people, events, dates, definitions, and so forth on the worksheet below.
2. Entries should be brief. Just record names, dates, an outline of events, short definitions, etc.
3. Save this sheet for your research. It will give you the background information you need to start your research. It may also trigger ideas about related subjects, people, events, and so on that will add depth and perspective to your investigation of the topic.

Key people	
Important dates	
History or development of the topic	
Important events	
Key words (words that might be useful to search under)	
Definitions (any concepts that add to your understanding)	
Current issues/events	
Other useful facts	

Lesson 3.7: Journals: Popular vs. Scholarly Periodicals

NAME: _____ DATE: _____

Journals and magazine are vitally important for current information in all disciplines. However, scholarly journals greatly differ from popular magazines. So, how do you tell the difference?

The following are a few characteristics of a scholarly journal:

- Have a serious look; often contain graphs and charts, but not exciting pictures
- Always cite their sources in the form of footnotes or bibliographies
- Articles are written by scholars in the field
- The language is that of the discipline covered and may be foreign to you
- Reports on original research or experimentation
- Many are published by professional organizations

The following are a few characteristics of a popular magazine:

- Lots of graphics—exciting photographs and drawings
- Usually slick and attractive in appearance
- Rarely cite sources
- Information is many times second- or third-hand
- Articles are short and written in simple language
- Main purpose is to entertain the reader

For this lesson, list five scholarly journals and five popular magazines that might be useful for your research topic.

YOUR TOPIC: _____

JOURNALS   MAGAZINES

1.   1.

2.   2.

3.   3.

4.   4.

5.   5.

From *An Educator's Guide to Information Literacy: What Every High School Senior Needs to Know*. Westport, CT: Libraries Unlimited, 2007. Copyright © 2007 by Ann Marlow Riedling.

Lesson 3.8: Primary and Secondary Sources

NAME: _____ DATE: _____

What is the difference between primary and secondary resources and why is it important? Primary sources (also called original research articles) allow the researcher to get as close as possible to what actually happened during a time period or an historical event. Primary sources were either created during the time period being studied or were created at a later date by a participant in the events being studied, and reflect the viewpoint of the participant or observer. Primary sources often appear in scholarly or peer-reviewed journals. A secondary resource is a work that interprets or analyzes an historical event or phenomenon. Secondary sources review articles and books; they are usually at least one step removed from the event.

To confirm that information came from a primary source, ask the following questions:

1. Does it include materials and methods for conducting the research?
2. Does it give every detail of the results?
3. Does it provide complete references?

Examples of primary sources include memoirs, letters, interviews, autobiographies, manuscript collections, speeches, photographs, audio and video recordings, and public opinion polls.

Some characteristics/examples of secondary sources are:

• They quote researchers from oral interviews
• Usually do not cite complete reference information

Examples of secondary sources are books, popular magazines, and letters to the editor.

For this lesson, list five primary and five secondary sources that may include information about your research topic.

YOUR TOPIC: _____

PRIMARY   SECONDARY

1.   1.

2.   2.

3.   3.

4.   4.

5.   5.

Lesson 3.9: Thesis Statements

NAME: _____ DATE: _____

A thesis statement declares what you intend to prove with your research. A good thesis statement makes the difference between a thoughtful research project and a simple retelling of facts. A thesis statement will help you focus your search for information. Before determining a thesis statement, you must do a great deal of background research and reading about your topic. Typically, a thesis statement is located at the end of your opening paragraph. It should be clear, strong, and easy to locate.

Some attributes of a good thesis statement are:

- Proposes an arguable point; takes a stand and justifies what you present
- Can be adequately covered in the format of the project assigned or chosen
- Is specific and focused
- Clearly asserts your own conclusion based on evidence
- Provides the readers with map to guide them through your work
- Avoids vague language and the first person

For this lesson, formulate a good thesis statement for your topic.

An example of a good thesis statement is:

Because half of all crack babies are likely to grow up in homes lacking good cognitive and emotional stimulation, the federal government should finance programs to supplement parental care for crack kids.

TOPIC: _____

THESIS STATEMENT: _____

DESCRIBE HOW YOU DEVELOPED YOUR THESIS STATEMENT:

From *An Educator's Guide to Information Literacy: What Every High School Senior Needs to Know*. Westport, CT: Libraries Unlimited, 2007. Copyright © 2007 by Ann Marlow Riedling.

Lessons for Standard 2

Standard 2 is as follows: The information literate student accesses needed information effectively and efficiently.

Performance Indicators: The information literate student selects the most appropriate investigative methods or information retrieval systems for accessing the needed information.

Outcomes include:

- Identifies appropriate investigative methods (e.g., laboratory experiment, simulation, fieldwork)
- Investigates benefits and applicability of various investigative methods
- Investigates the scope, content, and organization of information retrieval systems
- Selects efficient and effective approaches for accessing the information needed from the investigative method or information retrieval system

The information literate student constructs and implements effectively designed search strategies.

Outcomes include:

- Develops a research plan appropriate to the investigative method
- Identifies key words, synonyms, and related terms for the information needed
- Selects controlled vocabulary specific to the discipline or information retrieval source
- Constructs a search strategy using appropriate commands for the information retrieval system selected (e.g., Boolean operators, truncation, and proximity for search engines; internal organizers such as indexes for books)
- Implements the search strategy in various information retrieval systems using different user interfaces and search engines, with different command languages, protocols, and search parameters
- Implements the search using investigative protocols appropriate to the discipline

The information literate student retrieves information online or in person using a variety of methods.

Outcomes include:

- Uses various search systems to retrieve information in a variety of formats
- Uses various classification schemes and other systems (e.g., call number systems or indexes) to locate information resources within the library or to identify specific sites for physical exploration
- Uses specialized online or in-person services available at the institution to retrieve information needed (e.g., interlibrary loan/document delivery, professional associations, institutional research offices, community resources, experts and practitioners)
- Uses surveys, letters, interviews, and other forms of inquiry to retrieve primary information

The information literate student refines the search strategy if necessary.
Outcomes include:

- Assesses the quantity, quality, and relevance of the search results to determine whether alternative retrieval systems or investigative methods should be utilized
- Identifies gaps in the information retrieved and determines if the search strategy should be revised
- Repeats the search using the revised strategy as necessary

The information literate student extracts, records, and manages the information and its sources.
Outcomes include:

- Selects among various technologies the most appropriate one for the task of extracting the needed information (e.g., copy/paste software functions, photocopier, scanner, audio/visual equipment, or exploratory instruments)
- Creates a system for organizing the information
- Differentiates between the types of sources cited and understands the elements and correct syntax of a citation for a wide range of resources
- Records all pertinent citation information for future reference
- Uses various technologies to manage the information selected and organized

Lesson 3.10: Search Strategy

TOPIC WORKSHEET

Jot down a topic you would like to explore on the Web: _____

BEGIN THE PRE-SEARCHING ANALYSIS

1. What unique words, distinctive names, abbreviations, or acronyms are associated with your topic?

2. What societies, organizations, or groups might have information on your subject?

3. What other words are likely to be in any Web documents on your topic?
   You may want to use AND or precede each by + [no space]

4. Do any of the words in #1 or #3 above belong in phrases or strings?
   Search these as a "phrase in quotes" (for example, "affirmative action" or "communicable diseases").

5. For any of the terms in #4 above, can you think of synonyms, variant spellings, or equivalent terms you would also accept in relevant documents?
   You may want to use OR.

6. What extraneous or irrelevant documents might these words pick up?

7. What broader terms could your topic be covered by?
   When browsing subject categories or searching sites of Webliographies or databases on your topic, try broader categories.

From *An Educator's Guide to Information Literacy: What Every High School Senior Needs to Know*. Westport, CT: Libraries Unlimited, 2007. Copyright © 2007 by Ann Marlow Riedling.

Lesson 3.11: Key Words/Phrases and Synonyms

NAME: _____ DATE: _____

After you have developed your research question/thesis statement you will begin to identify key words and phrases. Then you will use these and their synonyms to start searching resources for answers to your research question. A key word or phrase is the word(s) that the research question is about. They are important words in the question.

What is a Thesis?

A thesis statement states what you believe and what you intend to prove. A good thesis statement makes the difference between a thoughtful research project and a simple retelling of facts.

A good thesis will help you focus your search for information. It is important to do a lot of background reading so that you know enough about a subject to identify key questions. You may not know how you stand on an issue until you have examined the evidence. You will likely begin your research with a working or preliminary thesis, which you will continue to refine until you are certain of where the evidence leads.

The thesis statement is typically located at the end of your opening paragraph. The opening paragraph serves to set the context for the thesis.

Remember, your reader will be looking for your thesis. Make it clear, strong, and easy to find.

A good thesis:

- should propose an arguable point with which people could reasonably disagree. A strong thesis is provocative; it takes a stand and justifies the discussion you will present.
- tackles a subject that could be adequately covered in the format of the project assigned.
- is specific and focused. A strong thesis proves a point without discussing everything about it.
- clearly asserts your own conclusion based on evidence. Note: The evidence may lead you to a conclusion you didn't think you'd reach. It is perfectly acceptable to change your thesis.
- provides the reader with a map to guide him or her through your work.
- anticipates and refutes counterarguments.
- avoids vague language.
- avoids the first person.
- should pass the "So what?" or "Who cares?" test.

How do you know if you've got a solid thesis? Try these five tests:

- Does the thesis inspire a reasonable reader to ask "How?" or "Why?"?
- Would a reasonable reader not respond with "So what?" or "Who cares?"?
- Does the thesis avoid general phrasing and/or sweeping words such as all, none, or every?

From *An Educator's Guide to Information Literacy: What Every High School Senior Needs to Know*. Westport, CT: Libraries Unlimited, 2007. Copyright © 2007 by Ann Marlow Riedling.

- Does the thesis lead the reader toward the topic sentences—the subtopics needed to prove the thesis?
- Can the thesis be adequately developed in the required length of the paper or project?

If you cannot answer "yes" to these questions, what changes should you make for your thesis to pass these tests?

RESEARCH QUESTION: _____

Now, go back and circle the key words and phrases in your research question.

List four key words or phrases; then list synonyms for each key word or phrase.

KEY WORD OR PHRASE	SYNONYMS
1.	1.
2.	2.
3.	3.
4.	4.

Lesson 3.12: Web Searching Strategies

NAME: _____ DATE: _____

To locate sites on the Web that contain the information you require, you must use some basic searching strategies. These strategies include, for example, Boolean operators, truncation, phrase searching, field searching, and proximity searching.

Boolean Operators:
- AND: This narrows a search. Terms linked with AND must be present in a retrieved record.
  - Example: gangs AND violence
  - The information retrieved for this search query must include both the words gangs and violence.
- OR: OR expands a search. This is where you can enter synonyms for a term.
  - Example: aged OR elderly
  - Information on either/or both terms is retrieved.
- NOT: NOT narrows a search. It excludes information from the records retrieved.
  - Example: bandage NOT adhesive
  - You want information about bandaged but not the adhesive type.

Truncation:
- The use of a symbol to obtain various endings to the stem or root of a word is called truncation. Often the truncation symbol is an asterisk (*) but the symbol may vary from database to database.
  - Example: educat* retrieves education, educate, educator, educated, and so forth

Phrase Searching:
- This searching strategy allows you to search words as phrases. On the Web, the use of quotation marks (" ") is sometimes used to indicate a phrase.
  - Examples: "civil rights," "colon cancer," and so forth
  - The use of searching phrases often leads to the retrieval of more pertinent information than searching with single words linked with the Boolean operator AND.

Field Searching:
- On the Web, various search engines have the ability to search specific fields of Web pages or records. Some of the more common fields that can be searched include the URL, title, summary, images, links, and text. Different coding is used by different search engines. Searching in a specific field of a record can be a very useful feature.
  - Examples: title: slavery; title: African-American slaves

Proximity Searching:
- Sometimes a Web search engine allows the researcher to identify documents with phrases or words in close proximity to one another, thus increasing the chances of retrieving pertinent information. The most common proximity operator is the word NEAR.
  - Example: effects NEAR gangs

For this lesson, use all of the examples above with your research question; then describe your process and results.

RESEARCH QUESTION: _____

PROCESSES: _____

RESULTS: _____

Lesson 3.13: Information Seeking Strategies

NAME: _____ DATE: _____

By planning how to conduct research, you save time and discover where to look for the information needed. It is extremely important to locate information from a variety of sources and assess specific information within individual resources. The purpose and nature of your research frames the strategy to use and the kind of resources to consult. Determine the kind of resources based on aspects of your chosen topic. For example, current information is likely to be found in current periodicals, newspapers, and online databases. Geographical information is likely found in atlases, maps, gazetteers, and guidebooks. First-hand information may be found in primary sources, including interviews. The best source answers the exact research question or problem at the appropriate depth and breadth.

For this lesson, list five specific resources (of different types) that could be used for your research paper.

RESEARCH QUESTION: _____

RESOURCES

1.

2.

3.

4.

5.

Lesson 3.14: Location and Access

NAME: _____ DATE: _____

The following Web sites may assist you in locating appropriate information for your proposed research. Explore each one thoroughly, including all links. Number them.

- Finding Information: *Library and Information Skills Tutorial*: http://ccc.commnet.edu/libroot/freshyear/wrkbk.htm
- Finding Information in Books:
  - *Using the Parts of a Book*: http://www.teach-nology.com/worksheets/research/book/basic/index.html
  - *Using a Table of Contents*: http://www.teach-nology.com/worksheets/research/book/contents
  - *Using an Index for Information*: http://www.teach-nology.com/worksheets/research/book/basket/1/
- Finding Information in Periodicals: *Finding Journal and Magazine Articles:* http://www.lib.duke.edu/libguide/fi_journals.htm
- Finding Information on the Internet:
  - *Finding Information on the Internet: A Tutorial:* http://www.lib.berkeley.edu/TeachingLib/Guides/Internet/FindInfo.html
  - *Infopeople:* http://www.infopeople.org/finding.html
  - *Spider's Apprentice:* http://monash.com/spidap.html
- Finding Information Through Interviews: *Oral History Techniques and Procedures:* http://www.army.mil/cmh-pg/books/oral.htm

For this lesson, write a sentence about each Web site—its contents, usefulness, and so on.

RESEARCH QUESTION: _____

1.

2.

3.

4.

5.

6.

7.

8.

9.

From *An Educator's Guide to Information Literacy: What Every High School Senior Needs to Know*. Westport, CT: Libraries Unlimited, 2007. Copyright © 2007 by Ann Marlow Riedling.

Lesson 3.15: Creating a Search Strategy

NAME: _____ DATE: _____

It is always a good idea to think about your search before you begin. Create a search strategy by asking yourself this question: What do I want to do? Browse? Locate a specific piece of information? Retrieve everything I can on the subject?

Your answer will determine how you conduct your search and what tools you will use.

- Browse: If you are browsing and trying to determine what is available in your subject area, begin by selecting a subject director such as Yahoo! Then, enter your key word(s) into one of the metasearch engines such as Vivisimo.
- Specific Information: If you are looking for specific pieces of information, go to a major search engine such as MSN or Google. Or to a specialized database such as the Bureau of the Census.
- Retrieve It All: If you want to retrieve everything you can on a subject, try the same search on several search engines. Also check books, newspapers, journals, and other print and non-print reference resources.

For this lesson, determine your search strategy and locate 10 resources that are appropriate for your research paper.

RESEARCH QUESTION: _____

RESOURCES

1.

2.

3.

4.

5.

6.

7.

8.

9.

10.

From *An Educator's Guide to Information Literacy: What Every High School Senior Needs to Know*. Westport, CT: Libraries Unlimited, 2007. Copyright © 2007 by Ann Marlow Riedling.

Lesson 3.16: Choosing the Best Search Engine

For this lesson, look at all sites listed in the URL below. Then write down the ones you would use for your research topic and why.

http://www.noodletools.com/debbie/literacies/information/5locate/adviceengine.html

Copyright granted by Debbie Abilock, NoodleTools, Inc. http://www.noodletools.com/debbie/consult/collab/f3pickatool.pdf [2004].

Lesson 3.17: How to Choose a Search Engine or Directory

- Fields and File Types
- Search Logic
- Search Options
- Search Results
- Speciality Searches

Fields & File Types	
If you want to search for...	*Choose...*
Audio/music	AllTheWeb	AltaVista	Dogpile	Fazzle	FindSounds.com	Lycos Music Downloads	Lycos Multimedia Search	Singingfish
Date last modified	AllTheWeb Advanced Search	AltaVista Advanced Web Search	Ask.com Advanced Search	Exalead Advanced Search	Google Advanced Search	HotBot Advanced Search	Yahoo Advanced Web Search
Domain/site/URL	AllTheWeb Advanced Search	AltaVista Advanced Web Search	AOL Advanced Search	Ask.com Advanced Search	Google Advanced Search	Lycos Advanced Search	MSN Search Search Builder	SearchEdu.com	Yahoo Advanced Web Search
File format	AllTheWeb Advanced Web Search	AltaVista Advanced Web Search	AOL Advanced Search	Exalead Advanced Search	Yahoo Advanced Web Search
Geographic location	Ask.com Advanced Search	Exalead Advanced Search	HotBot Advanced Search	Lycos Advanced Search	MSN Search Search Builder	Yahoo Advanced Web Search
Images	AllTheWeb	AltaVista	The Amazing Picture Machine	Ask.com Images	Ditto	Dogpile	Fazzle	Google Image Search	IceRocket	Ixquick	Mamma	Picsearch

Language	AllTheWeb Advanced Web Search	AOL Advanced Search	Ask.com Advanced Search	Exalead Advanced Search	Google Language Tools	HotBot Advanced Search	iBoogie Advanced Web Search	Lycos Advanced Search	MSN Search Search Builder	Yahoo Advanced Web Search
Multimedia and video	All TheWeb	AltaVista	Dogpile	Fazzle	IceRocket	Search For Video	Singingfish	Yahoo Video Search
Page title/URL	AOL Advanced Search	Fazzle	Google Advanced Search	Yahoo Advanced Web Search	ZapMeta Advanced Web Search

Search Logic

If you want to use…	*Choose…*
Boolean operators	AltaVista Advanced Web Search	AllTheWeb Advanced Search	Dogpile	Google [OR only]	Ixquick
Full Boolean logic with parentheses (e.g., *behavior and (cats or felines)*)	AlltheWeb Advanced Search	AltaVista Advanced Web Search	Exalead	Ixquick	MSN Search
Implied Boolean +/-	Most search engines offer this option
Boolean logic using search form terminology	Most advanced search options offer this, including: AllTheWeb Advanced Search	AltaVista Advanced Web Search AOL Advanced Search	Ask.com Advanced Search	Exalead	Google Advanced Search	IceRocket Advanced Search	MSN Search Search Builder	Yahoo Advanced Web Search
Proximity searching	Exalead	Google [by default]	Ixquick

Search Options

If you want..	*Choose…*
Alternative search terms	SurfWax
A user fill-in search form	Many search engines offer this, including: AlltheWeb Advanced Web Search	AltaVista Advanced Web Search	AOL Search Advanced Search	Ask.com Advanced Search	Google Advanced Search	IceRocket Advanced Search	MSN Search Builder	Yahoo Advanced Web Search

From *An Educator's Guide to Information Literacy: What Every High School Senior Needs to Know*. Westport, CT: Libraries Unlimited, 2007. Copyright © 2007 by Ann Marlow Riedling.

Search for documents similar to those in existing results	Google
Truncation	Exalead | Ixquick
Your search stated in plain English	Ask Jeeves | Brainboost | Ixquick | MSN Search
Translation of pages retrieved as search results, or any text or Web page, to and from selected languages	Babel Fish
An exact phrase within quotations	Most search engines offer this option
An exact phrase from a template choice	Many search templates offer this, including: AllTheWeb Advanced Search | AltaVista Advanced Web Search | Fazzle | Google Advanced Search | IceRocket Advanced Search
Multiple search tools searched simultaneously with duplicate records removed	Chubba | Clusty | Copernic | Don Busca | Fazzle | Ixquick | Mamma | MetaCrawler | Query Server | SurfWax | Yooci | more…

Search Results

If you want…	*Choose…*
Results based on linking (i.e., number of links from highly rated Web pages)	A9 | Alexa Web Search | AltaVista | Ask.com | Google | Google Web Directory [Many search engines use this technology as part of their results ranking strategy.]
Results clustered by concept and/or type of site (a "horizontal" in addition to a single vertical list of results)	Accumo | All 4 One MetaSearch | Clusty | Don Busca | Exalead | iBoogie | Infonetware | metaEUREEKA | Kartoo | KillerInfo | Mooter | Teoma | Turbo10 | Ujiko | Vivisimo
Option to search on related topics	AllTheWeb | Dogpile | Factbites
Clustering of results into one hit per site with the option to see all	AllTheWeb | AltaVista
Results in graphical format	Kartoo | Mooter | Ujiko
Results with thumbnail images of retrieved sites	Don Busca | Exalead | IceRocket
Queries stored at the site and notification of new results	Google Alert | Karnak | TracerLock
Queries stored by the search service for repeat searches	Copernic

Specialty Searches

If you want to search…	Choose…
The Deep Web (not generally covered by search spiders)	Complete Planet | Google | Search.Com | Turbo10
	[Many search engine sites offer deep Web searches. For example, see Ixquick and InfoGrid]
Blogs	Blogdex | Blogdigger | Bloglines | BlogPulse | Bloogz | Clusty | Daypop | Feedster | Globe of Blogs | Google Blog Search | IceRocket | Technorati | Yahoo News Search
Files in FTP sites (text, multimedia, software, etc.)	FileIndexer.com | Ftpsearchengines.com | Oth Net
News (multiple sources searched simultaneously)	AlltheWeb: News | AltaVista - News | FindNews.org | Google News Alerts | InfoGrid | NewsNow | NewsTrove.com | Pandia Newsfinder | RocketNews | Topix.net | The WorldNews Network
News (RSS feeds)	Daypop | Memigo | NewsIsFree
RSS feeds	2RSS.com | Chordata | Daypop | Feed-Directory.com | RSSfeeds.com | SurfWax LookAhead | Syndic8.com
Saved Web pages	Furl | Spurl.net
Scholarly materials	Google Book Search | Google Scholar | Open WorldCat | Windows Live Academic
Search trails (e.g., paths taken from search results to selected pages)	Trexy
Site analysis	GoLexa
Usenet newsgroup postings	Google Groups
Reference sources (dictionaries, encyclopedias, e-mail and address lookups, calculators, quotations, news, government info, statistics etc.)	Reference Collection
Professionally maintained directories	About | Academic Info | BUBL LINK | INFOMINE | Librarians' Internet Index | Resource Discovery Network | Scout Report Archives | Virtual Learning Resources Center | WWW Virtual Library | more…
Directories maintained by volunteers	JoeAnt | Open Directory Project (DMOZ)

Lesson 3.18: Seven-Step Research Process

NAME: _____ DATE: _____

The following is one example of a research process. Depending on your topic and the amount of information needed, you may need to rearrange or recycle these steps:

1. *Identify and Develop Your Topic*: State your topic as a question. Identify the key words in your question.
2. *Find Background Information*: Look up your key words in the indexes to subject encyclopedias. Read articles in these encyclopedias to set the context for your research. Additional background information may be found in your lecture notes, textbooks, reserve readings, and so forth.
3. *Use Catalogs to Find Books and Media*: Use key word searching for a narrow search; use subject searching for a broad search. Write down the complete citation and location information.
4. *Use Indexes to Find Periodical Articles*: Use periodical indexes and abstracts to locate citations to articles (ask your local librarian about which databases they have available). Choose the ones that are best suited to your topic.
5. *Find Internet Sources*: Use search engines, subject directories, and the invisible Web to locate information on the Internet.
6. *Evaluate What You Find*: It is critical that you evaluate the information you locate; in particular, the Internet. (See the next standard for additional information regarding evaluating the World Wide Web.)
7. *Cite What You Find Using a Standard Format*: Give credit where credit is due—cite your sources. Citing your sources serves two purposes, it gives proper credit to the creators of the materials used, and it allows those who read your work to duplicate your research and locate the sources you listed as references (additional information regarding citing sources can be found later in this chapter).

For this lesson, use all seven steps of this research process to locate appropriate information for your research. Write down pertinent thoughts as you proceed through this process.

RESEARCH QUESTION: _____

STEPS

1.

2.

3.

4.

5.

6.

7.

Lesson 3.19: Search Tools

For this lesson, please refer to the following URL: http://infopeople.org/search/.

Search Tools

- **Our Top Choices**
  - **Best Search Tools Page**—Search form with the best search tools on one page. Bookmark this page for efficient searching.
  - **Search Tools Chart**—Chart of the best features of the best search tools. Print this for yourself and your patrons. Available in PDF for printing to two pages.

- **Current News and Weather**
  - **Google News**—Information culled from approximately 4,500 news sources worldwide and automatically arranged to present the most relevant news first. Topics are updated continuously throughout the day. Trace the history of a developing issue by clicking the "sort by date" function on the page containing all reports on a given topic.
  - **NewsCenter: Up to the Minute News Resources**—This directory includes links for: major wire services; one-stop shops; search for news; U.S. news; business news; international news; technology; entertainment; and more.
  - **UM Weather (Weather Underground)**—The heart of the site is the Weather Underground database of weather conditions and forecasts from around the globe, as well as hard to find daily historic weather records (most dating back six years).
  - **Yahoo! News**—Excellent resource getting information from more than 7,000 sources. News briefs are updated throughout the day with fuller coverage of some stories. Includes geographic categories—world, national, and local. Other topics include business, technology, health, entertainment, science, and sports. Many topics have links to related Web sites. Check out the advanced search form!

- **Government Information**
  - **California State Home Page**
  - **Consumer.gov**—Federal government gateway to consumer information.
  - **FCIC National Contact Center**—Starting point for federal programs, benefits, or services.
  - **FedForms**—One-stop-shopping for forms needed for the top 500 government services used by the public.
  - **FirstGov.gov**—Portal to federal government information.
  - **healthfinder.gov**—Federal government gateway to health information.
  - **Local Governments**—Gateway to local government information (United States).

- **Indexes:**
  - **Librarians' Internet Index**—Searchable, evaluated, and annotated subject directory of Internet resources selected for their usefulness to the public library user's information needs. The indexers are California librarians.
  - **Infomine: Scholarly Internet Resource Collections**—Selected and described links to scholarly resources on the Internet. Searchable within each major topic. Maintained by librarians from various California universities.

From *An Educator's Guide to Information Literacy: What Every High School Senior Needs to Know*. Westport, CT: Libraries Unlimited, 2007. Copyright © 2007 by Ann Marlow Riedling.

- **Job Hunting**
  - **The Riley Guide: Employment Opportunities and Job Resources on the Internet**—The guide to job information.
  - **JobStar: California Job Search Guide**—Now covers Los Angeles, Sacramento, and San Diego, as well as the Bay Area. Includes a salary information section, which has 200+ links to online surveys. If you're looking for a job in California, start here.

- **Kids**
  - **Children's Literature Web Guide**—Internet resources related to books for children and young adults. Excellent source!
  - **The Internet Advocate**—Resource guide for librarians and educators who want to use the Internet with kids. Includes a special section on developing an Acceptable Use Policy (AUP).
  - **KidsClick!**—Searchable and browsable directory of Internet resources selected, evaluated, and annotated by children's librarians. Fantastic resource! Communications regarding the KidsClick! project can be directed to: kclick@sunsite.berkeley.edu.

- **Ready Reference Collection**—Excellent, annotated collection, from the Internet Public Library.
- **Refdesk.com**—Links to ready reference sites with everything from college rankings to a zip code finder, as well as encyclopedias, headline news, and more.

Permission granted by Linda Rodenspiel, 2006, Source: Infopeople.

Lesson 3.20: Internet Subject Directories

NAME: _____ DATE: _____

Subject directories are Internet sites that organize information by topic. When you use a subject directory, you are not searching the entire Internet; you are only searching for Web sites that have been assigned a specific topic by librarians, subject experts, and other individuals. Some subject directories contain as many as 50,000 Web sites; others are quite small. Many have a hierarchical arrangement, which means you start out with a broad topic and narrow it as you click your way through the database. Subject directories provide access to more reliable sites that more closely relate to the topic you are researching. These Web sites have been reviewed and will typically be more acceptable for research. There are a few commercial subject directories such as Yahoo! and Open Directory; these are also organized by topic, but because the sites are not as carefully screened, you will need to evaluate them more carefully.

Using the following subject directories, see if you can locate information regarding your research topic:

1. Librarian's Index to the Internet: http://lii.org
2. Infomine: http://infomine.ucr.edu
3. Academic Information: http://www.academicinfo.net

RESEARCH TOPIC: _____

1.

2.

3.

Lessons for Standard 3

Standard 3 is as follows: The information literate student evaluates information and its sources critically and incorporates selected information into his or her knowledge base and value system.

Performance Indicators: The information literate student summarizes the main ideas to be extracted from the information gathered.

Outcomes include:

- Reads the text and selects main ideas
- Restates textual concepts in his or her own words and selects data accurately
- Identifies verbatim material that can be appropriately quoted

The information literate student articulates and applies initial criteria for evaluating both the information and its sources.

Outcomes include:

- Examines and compares information from various sources in order to evaluate reliability, validity, accuracy, authority, timeliness, and point of view or bias
- Analyzes the structure and logic of supporting arguments or methods
- Recognizes prejudice, deception, or manipulation
- Recognizes the cultural, physical, or other context within which the information was created and understands the impact of context on interpreting the information

The information literate student synthesizes main ideas to construct new concepts.
Outcomes include:

- Recognizes interrelationships among concepts and combines them into potentially useful primary statements with supporting evidence
- Extends initial synthesis, when possible, at a higher level of abstraction to construct new hypotheses that may require additional information
- Utilizes computer and other technologies (e.g., spreadsheets, databases, multimedia, and audio or visual equipment) for studying the interaction of ideas and other phenomena

The information literate student compares new knowledge with prior knowledge to determine the value added, contradictions, or other unique characteristics of the information.

Outcomes include:

- Determines whether information satisfies the research or other information need
- Uses consciously selected criteria to determine whether the information contradicts or verifies information used from other sources
- Draws conclusions based upon information gathered
- Tests theories with discipline-appropriate techniques (e.g., simulators, experiments)

- Determines probable accuracy by questioning the source of the data, the limitations of the information gathering tools or strategies, and the reasonableness of the conclusions
- Integrates new information with previous information or knowledge
- Selects information that provides evidence for the topic

The information literate student determines whether the new knowledge has an impact on the individual's value system and takes steps to reconcile differences.
Outcomes include:

- Investigates differing viewpoints encountered in the literature
- Determines whether to incorporate or reject viewpoints encountered

The information literate student validates understanding and interpretation of the information through discourse with other individuals, subject-area experts, and/or practitioners.
Outcomes include:

- Participates in classroom and other discussions
- Participates in class-sponsored electronic communication forums designed to encourage discourse on the topic (e.g., e-mail, bulletin boards, chat rooms)
- Seeks expert opinion through a variety of mechanisms (e.g., interviews, e-mail, listservs)

The information literate student determines whether the initial query should be revised.
Outcomes include:

- Determines if original information need has been satisfied or if additional information is needed
- Reviews search strategy and incorporates additional concepts as necessary
- Reviews information retrieval sources used and expands to include others as needed

Lesson 3.21: The Internet: An Overview

NAME: _____ DATE: _____

For this lesson, answer the following questions. (This may be done individually, in small or large groups.)

- Do you currently use the Internet for research? Why or why not?

- Do you rank the Internet or a school or public library as the best source of information? Why did you choose what you did?

- What are the advantages of the Internet over other resources?

- What are the disadvantages of the Internet over other resources?

- What is the difference between publishing information on the Internet and publishing information in books?

- How much of the information you find on the Internet do you think is true and can be trusted? Why?

- Currently, what do you do to check that the information you find on the Internet is reliable?

Lesson 3.22: Evaluating Web Pages

NAME: _____ DATE: _____

Evaluating Web pages skillfully requires that you train your eyes and fingers to employ a series of techniques that help you find what you need to know and train your mind to think critically to help you decide how much a Web page can be trusted. The following are tips and techniques to assist you in locating valid, reliable, unbiased information on the Internet.

1. Look for a personal name following a tilde (~) or a percent sign (%) in the URL.
2. Look at the domain for .edu, .gov, .org, .com, .net, or a foreign country code in the URL.
3. Look between the http:// and the first / to discover who published the site why this is important.
4. Look for links that say, "Philosophy," "Background," "About Us," "Biography"—look for bias.
5. Look for the date "last updated"—usually at the bottom of the home page.
6. Look for the name of the author, organization, institution, agency, or whoever is responsible for the site.
7. Look for the author's or creator's credentials to verify reliability and quality.
8. Look at the links to see if they add valid information or not.
9. Look for any items that point to irony, fraud, or falsehood.
10. Look for why the page was put on the Web—to give facts, persuade, sell, etc.

For this lesson, look at three Web sites that may be applicable to your research topic and evaluate each site using the information above.

RESEARCH TOPIC: _____

Site 1	Site 2	Site 3
1.		
2.		
3.		
4.		
5.		
6.		
7.		
8.		
9.		
10.		

Lesson 3.23: Evaluate a Web Site

NAME: _____ DATE: _____

Evaluate the following Web site using the questions below:

Smoking from All Sides: http://smokingsides.com

1. Who is the author or creator of this Web site?

2. What are the mission, goals, and objectives of this site?

3. When was the site last updated?

4. Do the graphics, images, and sounds, if applicable, enhance the Web site?

5. Who is the intended target audience?

6. Does the Web site contain contact information for your comments?

7. Does the site include references and credentials? What does this tell you?

Lesson 3.24: A Closer Look at Web Sites

NAME: _____ DATE: _____

For this lesson, thoroughly explore each Web site listed below. Then write a minimum of three sentences describing the site and whether you believe it is useful (and why or why not). How about valid or reliable?

1. NetLingo—The Internet Directory: http://www.netlingo.com.
2. Noodle Tools: Information Literacy: Search Strategies: http://www.noodletools.com/debbie/literacies/information/5locate/adviceengine.html
3. Search Engine Watch: http://www.searchenginewatch.com
4. Guide to Effective Searching of the Internet: http://www.brightplanet.com/deepcontent/tutorials/search/index.asp
5. The Web: Teaching Zack to Think: http://www.media-awareness.ca/english/resources/educational/handouts/internet/teaching_zack.cfm

1.

2.

3.

4.

5.

Lesson 3.25: Web Evaluation

NAME: _____ DATE: _____

Using the following web evaluation sheet, evaluate www.tecsoc.org.

Web Evaluation for Secondary Grades

Developed by Tammy Payton

Return to [Evaluation Design] [Teaching Resources] [West Home Page]

Name of site _____ Date: _____

URL: _____ Time _____ A.M./P.M.

1 = Poor 5 =Exceptional

Design

Navigability is good. Links are clearly labeled.
Can move from page to page easily.   1   2   3   4   5

This site offers interactivity.
The visitor engages with the site.   1   2   3   4   5

This site uses appropriate page format.
Pages are not inordinately long.   1   2   3   4   5

Can easily find information.   1   2   3   4   5

This site is aesthetically appealing.
Good use of graphics and color.   1   2   3   4   5

This site is aesthetically courteous.
Text and background colors do not clash.   1   2   3   4   5

Content

Has a proper title.   1   2   3   4   5

Additional resource links are included.   1   2   3   4   5

Information is useful.   1   2   3   4   5

Rich content and will likely be revisited.   1   2   3   4   5

How this Web site compares in content to similar Web sites.   1   2   3   4   5

From *An Educator's Guide to Information Literacy: What Every High School Senior Needs to Know*. Westport, CT: Libraries Unlimited, 2007. Copyright © 2007 by Ann Marlow Riedling.

Technical Elements

All links work.   1   2   3   4   5

Thumbnail graphics used. Graphics download quickly.   1   2   3   4   5

Alternative text page is offered when heavy
graphics or frames are used.   1   2   3   4   5

Image links and image maps have a text alternative.   1   2   3   4   5

Can see meaningful information within 30 seconds.   1   2   3   4   5

Credibility

Contact person is stated with his or her e-mail address.   1   2   3   4   5

Announces when this page was last updated.
Links have been kept current.   1   2   3   4   5

Resource links used to develop content are included.   1   2   3   4   5

States the name of the host school or institution.   1   2   3   4   5

Total Possible Points = 100

Permission granted by Tammy Payton, 2006, www.tammypayton.net/courses/print/evalweb2.shtml.

Lesson 3.26: Evaluation of Information Sources

NAME: _____ DATE: _____

View the following Web sites regarding evaluation. Write one paragraph about each explaining what you learned by visiting each site.

1. Criteria for Evaluation of Internet Information Sources: http://www.vuw.ac.nz/staff/alastair_smith/evaln/index.htm
2. Critical Evaluation of Resources: http://www.lib.berkeley.edu/TeachingLib/Guides/Evaluation.html
3. Current Web Contents Web Site Selection Criteria: http://scientific.thomson.com/free/essays/selectionofmaterial/cwc-criteria/
4. Evaluate Web Pages: http://www.widener.edu/Tools_Resources/Libraries/Wolfgram_Memorial_Library/Evaluate_Web_Pages/659/
5. Evaluating Internet Research Sources: http://www.virtualsalt.com/evalu8it.htm
6. The Good, The Bad & The Ugly: http://lib.nmsu.edu/instruction/evalcrit.html
7. Critically Analyzing Information Sources: http://www.library.cornell.edu/olinuris/ref/research/skill26.htm

What you learned (one paragraph per Web site):

1.

2.

3.

4.

5.

6.

7.

Lesson 3.27: Search Engines

NAME: _____ DATE: _____

For this lesson, once again browse the following Web sites. Critique each site (no more than five sentences):

1. How to Choose a Search Engine or Directory: http://library.albany.edu/internet/choose.html
2. Choosing the Best Search Engine for Your Information Need: http://www.noodletools.com/debbie/literacies/information/5locate/adviceengine.html
3. Search Engines Quick Guide: http://www.infopeople.org/search/guide.html
4. Search Engine Chart: http://www.infopeople.org/search/chart.html
5. Why Should I Take This Author Seriously?: http://mciu.org/~spjvweb/whyauthor.html

Your Critique:

1.

2.

3.

4.

5.

From *An Educator's Guide to Information Literacy: What Every High School Senior Needs to Know*. Westport, CT: Libraries Unlimited, 2007. Copyright © 2007 by Ann Marlow Riedling.

Lessons for Standard 4

Standard 4 is as follows: The information literate student, individually or as a member of a group, uses information effectively to accomplish a specific purpose.

Performance Indicators: The information literate student applies new and prior information to the planning and creation of a particular product or performance.

Outcomes include:

- Organizes the content in a manner that supports the purposes and format of the product or performance (e.g., outlines, drafts, storyboards)
- Articulates knowledge and skills transferred from prior experiences to planning and creating the product or performance
- Integrates the new and prior information, including quotations and paraphrasings, in a manner that supports the purposes of the product or performance
- Manipulates digital text, images, and data, as needed, transferring them from their original locations and formats to a new context

The information literate student revises the development process for the product or performance.

Outcomes include:

- Maintains a journal or log of activities related to the information seeking, evaluating, and communicating process
- Reflects on past successes, failures, and alternative strategies

The information literate student communicates the product or performance effectively to others.

Outcomes include:

- Chooses a communication medium and format that best supports the purposes of the product and the intended audience
- Uses a range of information technology applications in creating the product or performance
- Incorporates principles of design and communication
- Communicates clearly and with a style that supports the purposes of the intended audience

Lesson 3.28: Note-Taking

NAME: _____ DATE: _____

http://www.kernhigh.org/district/instruct/InformationLiteracy/Using_Info/5a_notetaking_%20final.htm.

Following the Cornell System of note-taking, use your research topic and follow the directions provided.

Note-taking—THE CORNELL SYSTEM

The Cornell system for taking notes is designed to save time but yet be highly efficient. There is no rewriting or retyping of your notes. It is a "DO IT RIGHT IN THE FIRST PLACE" system.

1. First Step—PREPARATION

Use a large, loose-leaf notebook. Use only one side of the paper (you then can lay your notes out to see the direction of a lecture). Draw a vertical line 2 1/2 inches from the left side of you paper. This is the recall column. Notes will be taken to the right of this margin. Later key words or phrases can be written in the recall column.

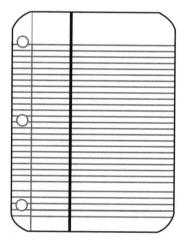

2. Second Step—TAKING NOTES FROM SOURCES

Record notes in paragraph form using YOUR OWN WORDS. Capture general ideas—summarizing, paraphrasing, or quoting main points. Put quotation marks around direct quotes. Skip lines to show the end of ideas or thoughts. Using abbreviations will save time (see "Simple Abbreviations" on the following page). Write legibly.

- *Summarize* means to briefly explain the information in your own words. A summary condenses the content of a lengthy passage. When you write a summary, you reformulate the main idea and outline the main points that support it.
- *Paraphrase* means to restate the content of a short passage. When you write a paraphrase, you reconstruct the passage phrase by phrase, recasting the author's words in your own.

- *Quote* means to use the exact words of the author. Quotes are enclosed in quotation marks.

3. Third Step—AFTER TAKING NOTES

Read through your notes and make them more legible if necessary. Now use the column. Jot down ideas or key words from your notes. Also, write any questions you may have. The information in the left-hand column may be used for arranging your notes according to topic before writing your paper or for organizing information before creating Power-Point slides or a pamphlet.

Simple Abbreviations

+	and	4	for
>	increase	2	to
<	decrease	&	or/and
w/	with	-	minus less
w/o	without	=	equals
w/I	within	≠	diff/not equal
ø	no, not ever	prt	part
b	be	b/w	between
i.e.	that is	Symbols	! @ # $ % > <

Additional Suggestions:

- Use symbols, diagrams, or drawings to simplify ideas. Example: Draw arrows to show connections between ideas.
- Make names and titles into acronyms after writing them once.
- Write first few syllables of long words and complete the word when reviewing notes.
    - ~ collect coll   ~ communicate comm
- Write words deleting vowels until notes are reviewed.
    - ~ speak spk   ~ communicate commnct   ~ community commnty

Can you think of some of your own short cuts?

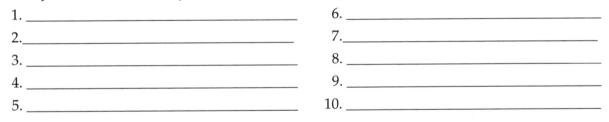

1. _____	6. _____
2. _____	7. _____
3. _____	8. _____
4. _____	9. _____
5. _____	10. _____

From Virginia Tech—Reading and Study Skills: Note-taking

http://www.ucc.vt.edu/stdysk/cornell.html

The information in this lesson focuses on taking notes from sources. The following sites have additional information on Cornell note-taking:

Cornell Note-taking System

http://www.mccallie.org/DaveHall/notes.html

http://www.byu.edu/stlife/cdc/Learning_Strategies/study_skills/note-tak.htm

Permission granted by Jim Jose, University of Newcastle, Callagan, NSW 2308 and the Support and Equity Branch of Charles Darwin University (formerly Northern Territory University), 2006.

From *An Educator's Guide to Information Literacy: What Every High School Senior Needs to Know*. Westport, CT: Libraries Unlimited, 2007. Copyright © 2007 by Ann Marlow Riedling.

Lesson 3.29: Note Making

NAME: _____ DATE: _____

Choose one of the ways you can take notes and do so with a minimum of three sources.

Note Layouts

There are numerous ways in which you can lay out your notes. Here are a few for you to explore:

- linear notes
- key word trees
- mind maps
- networks
- herringbone technique

Whichever note-making layout you choose to use, you may find it useful to use abbreviations and shortened versions of commonly used words. This will help you save time with writing so that you can concentrate on noting the essential point or idea. Some common abbreviations are listed below. Note that some common abbreviations can be used in more than one context.

Student Facilitator
jim.jose@ntu.edu.au

Copyright Information
Last Modified: Feb 2000

Permission granted by Jim Jose, University of Newcastle, Callaghan, NSW 2308 and the Support and Equity Branch of Charles Darwin University (formerly Northern Territory University), 2006.

Lesson 3.30: Paraphrasing a Source

NAME: _____ DATE: _____

Paraphrasing is one form of note-taking. Paraphrasing requires that you rewrite a passage in your own words, but still preserve the complete meaning of the passage. A brief definition of paraphrasing is as follows:

Information from a source that has been written in your own words, usually in more simplistic vocabulary and sentences. The body of writing is equal in length to the original body of information. The paraphrased version of information is easier to understand.

The following will help you with paraphrasing:

- Read the information you want to paraphrase completely through once, focusing on its meaning.
- Carefully choose what you want to paraphrase in the passage. (You don't need to paraphrase a whole section.) You may include a quote within your paraphrase; use quotation marks around the quoted material.
- Write the information down in your own words, taking care to preserve the complete meaning of the passage.
- Include the page number in parentheses at the end of any quote or paraphrase if you get the information from a book.

For this lesson, paraphrase the following passage:

The expatriate experience has shaped my life—and it is shaping the lives and careers of an increasing number of people as more organizations become international. Traditionally, expatriates share their experiences among themselves, but apart from this interaction, there are few resources—formal or informal—to help expatriates and potential expatriates make sense of the often radical changes that working abroad can make in their lives. I realized that such resources were needed when I repeatedly heard these questions from expatriates I interviewed: "Is my experience normal? Have you heard similar stories from other expatriates?" The realization that others have taken the same journey and pondered the same questions is comforting and makes the transition, first to overseas and then back home, more manageable, freeing the expatriate to focus more fully on his or her work.

Paraphrase:

Lesson 3.31: Quoting and Summarizing

NAME: _____ DATE: _____

You can borrow from the works of others as you research and write. Good writers use paraphrasing, quoting, and summarizing to blend materials in with their own, while making sure their own voice is heard.

Quotations are the exact words of an author, copied directly from the source (word-for-word). Quotations must be cited. Use quotations when:

- You want to add the power of an author's words to support your argument
- You want to disagree with an author's argument
- You want to highlight particularly eloquent or powerful phrases or passages
- You are comparing and contrasting specific points of view
- You want to note the important research that precedes your own

Summarizing involves putting the main idea(s) of one or more writers into your own words, including only the main point(s). It is necessary to attribute summarized ideas to the original source. Summarized ideas are not necessarily presented in the same order as in the original source. Summaries are significantly shorter than the original and take a broad overview of the source material. Summarize when:

- You want to establish background or offer an overview of a topic
- You want to describe common knowledge (from several sources) about a topic
- You want to determine the main ideas of a single source

For this lesson, summarize the following passage and select one sentence you would like to quote:

Everywhere I went in Oman I was met with friendship and hospitality, exuberance and pride, curiosity and zeal. And I discovered many other things:

- Oman, as a political entity, has been around longer than any other nation in the gulf region. Oman is older than the United States and extended its arm of friendship a good 20 years before the start of the American Civil War.
- Oman is a country whose underpinnings are, curiously enough, nurtured by democratic principles similar to our own.
- Oman is a country that calls upon all of its citizens to share the responsibility of carving out its own destiny; where outdated gender biases are put aside in a true spirit of cooperation.
- Oman has celebrated, in its long history, moments of greatness and, in the twentieth century, perhaps has weathered its darkest hour.

Summarize:

Quote:

Lesson 3.32: Online Databases

NAME: _____ DATE: _____

Online databases store information from reference books, magazines/journals, newspapers, primary sources, and sometimes even multimedia sources. Although they are accessed electronically, they are not the same as Internet sources. Rather, they are digitized print sources, which make their information searchable. There are many online databases; many for a fee. Ask your librarian to which ones they subscribe and what fields they research. Examples include: ProQuest, EBSCO, PubMed, and so forth. To search, enter key words or phrases (many times in quotation marks). These often use Boolean operators and truncation. Most databases will allow you to print, e-mail, or save your sources.

For this lesson, visit an academic or public library and determine what online databases they offer. Search them all, noting what field they are in, what they include, and any other permanent information. List five of them below:

Database	Field	Special Attributes
1.	1.	1.
2.	2.	2.
3.	3.	3.
4.	4.	4.
5.	5.	5.

Lesson 3.33: PowerPoint Presentations

NAME: _____ DATE: _____

For this lesson, explore the two Web sites listed below (both dealing with PowerPoint presentations). Write a critique of each site.

1. PowerPoint FAQ: http://www.bitbetter.com/powerfaq.htm
2. PowerPoint Tutorial: http://www.fgcu.edu/support/office2000/ppt

1.

2.

Lessons for Standard 5

Standard 5 is as follows: The information literate student understands many of the ethical, legal, and socioeconomic issues surrounding the use of information and accesses and uses information ethically and legally.

Performance Indicators: The information literate student understands many of the ethical, legal, and socioeconomic issues surrounding information and information technology.
Outcomes include:

- Identifies and discusses issues related to privacy and security in both the print and electronic environments
- Identifies and discusses issues related to free and fee-based access to information
- Identifies and discusses issues related to censorship and freedom of speech
- Demonstrates an understanding of intellectual property, copyright, and fair use of copyrighted material

The information literate student follows laws, regulations, institutional policies, and etiquette related to the access and use of information resources.
Outcomes include:

- Participates in electronic discussions following accepted practices (e.g., Netiquette)
- Uses approved passwords and other forms of ID for access to information resources
- Complies with institutional policies on access to information resources
- Preserves the integrity of information resources, equipment, systems, and facilities
- Legally obtains, stores, and disseminates text, data, images, or sounds
- Demonstrates an understanding of what constitutes plagiarism and does not represent work attributable to others as his or her own
- Demonstrates an understanding of institutional policies related to human subjects research

The information literate student acknowledges the use of information sources in communicating the product or performance.
Outcomes include:

- Selects an appropriate documentation style and uses it consistently to cite sources
- Posts permission-granted notices, as needed, for copyrighted material

Lesson 3.34: Cybercrime

NAME: _____ DATE: _____

Visit the following Web site: http://www.cybercrime.gov. Explore it thoroughly. Write a one-page overview of the site.

Lesson 3.35: Is It Plagiarism?

NAME: _____ DATE: _____

For this lesson, answer the questions provided below.

Is it plagiarism? A discussion

Ethics is doing the right thing even when no one is looking. Plagiarism is theft of intellectual property. It is a form of cheating or stealing. If you present the work of others—words, images, sounds, ideas—as your own, you are plagiarizing. As students you should be concerned about learning, and about developing habits of scholarship.

The most obvious form of plagiarism is stealing an author's exact words and failing to use quotation marks or to cite the author. However, plagiarism can be far more subtle. Many students plagiarize unintentionally.

In order to be sure you avoid plagiarism, you'll need to have a clear idea of exactly what might be considered plagiarism. Have you, or have you ever heard of anyone else actually doing any of these things? (No names, please.) Before we discuss these cases as a class, decide which of the following you would consider plagiarism. Some are clearer examples than others. Be ready to discuss your responses with the class.

Copying or sharing assignments Comments:	Yes	No	Not Sure
Failing to cite a commonly known source Comments:	Yes	No	Not Sure
Failing to cite a statistic Comments:	Yes	No	Not Sure
Paraphrasing the work of others you find in books, magazines, Web sites without documentation Comments:	Yes	No	Not Sure
Asking another student to write a paper for you Comments:	Yes	No	Not Sure
Copying material from another source, citing the material in your bibliography, but leaving out in-text documentation Comments:	Yes	No	Not Sure
Listing works in your bibliography that you have not used or read Comments:	Yes	No	Not Sure
Mixing the words of an author with your own without documentation Comments:	Yes	No	Not Sure

From *An Educator's Guide to Information Literacy: What Every High School Senior Needs to Know*. Westport, CT: Libraries Unlimited, 2007. Copyright © 2007 by Ann Marlow Riedling.

Taking a paper you wrote for one class and submitting it to another teacher Comments:	Yes	No	Not Sure
Having your parent substantially edit your work Comments:	Yes	No	Not Sure
Copying and pasting relevant pieces of electronic text together as you research, citing as you go along Comments:	Yes	No	Not Sure
Copying and pasting relevant pieces of electronic text together as you research without citing Comments:	Yes	No	Not Sure
Presenting a paper or document you found on the Internet as your own Comments:	Yes	No	Not Sure
Substantially editing a paper you found on the Internet Comments:	Yes	No	Not Sure
When collaborating with other students, changing papers slightly to make each one a little different Comments:	Yes	No	Not Sure
Pasting an image from a Web site into your multimedia project and documenting it Comments:	Yes	No	Not Sure
Pasting an image from a Web site into your Web page and documenting it Comments:	Yes	No	Not Sure

Permission granted by Joyce Valenza, 2006.

Lesson 3.36: Avoiding Plagiarism

NAME: _____ DATE: _____

Tips About How To Avoid Plagiarism:

- When you are taking notes, make sure that you copy all original passages in quotation marks.
- Paraphrase by really putting ideas into your own words; go beyond changing a few words. Recognize that paraphrasing of unique ideas and facts also requires citations.
- As you write, return to the text and check your paraphrase against the original source to make sure you haven't unintentionally copied.
- Use graphic organizers to restructure your facts and ideas.
- Use your own voice to put a new twist on old information.
- When in doubt, cite!

Common Knowledge:

- You don't have to cite everything. Facts or ideas referred to as common knowledge do not have to be cited.
- Common knowledge includes facts that are found in many sources, facts that you assume many people know. A rule of thumb is that if you find a fact in three or more sources, it may be considered common knowledge.
- An example of common knowledge is that President George W. Bush has two daughters.

Remember, you must document little-known facts and any ideas that interpret facts even if they are paraphrased.

For this lesson, exchange something you have written for a class with another person. Look it over and decide if there is evident plagiarism, examples of common knowledge, and so forth.

From *An Educator's Guide to Information Literacy: What Every High School Senior Needs to Know*. Westport, CT: Libraries Unlimited, 2007. Copyright © 2007 by Ann Marlow Riedling.

Lesson 3.37: Internet Ethics

NAME: _____ DATE: _____

For this lesson, answer the questions provided.

Zippy Scenarios for Teaching Internet Ethics

Note to educators: Feel free to use any of the following scenarios for educational purposes. And please feel free to share your own ideas too!

Describe the underlying Netiquette/ethics issue(s) in each scenario. What is your opinion of the behaviors involved? What equitable solutions can you suggest? Describe a parallel situation in which computers are NOT involved.

1. Jules has walked away from a lab computer without logging off. Trish sits down and, still logged in as Jules, sends inflammatory e-mail messages out to a number of students and posts similar messages on the class newsgroup.
2. Lester sends e-mail to the entire student body inviting them to a BYOB party at his house while his parents are out of town. Lester receives a message from a system administrator calling him in for a meeting with school officials. He objects because he feels that his e-mail is his own private business.
3. Every time Abner posts a comment to a newsgroup, his posts are flamed by a group of "enemies." Abner has responded to each flame in turn, and a full-scale war is now in progress.
4. It seems like every time Melanie logs on to her account, Stanley knows about it and sends messages that cover her screen with text. At first she thinks it is funny, but now it's really starting to bother her. The messages reformat the text on her screen and, besides, it's kind of creepy the way he always knows she's logged on.
5. Sharon and Timothy are students at Big Suburban High School. They have designed a Web page devoted to their favorite rock band using their personal disk space on the school's Web server. They have posted song clips, lyrics, photographs of each band member, and articles they have found in various Web news sources. However, school authorities have asked them to shut down their site because of the obscene content of many of the lyrics. Sharon and Timothy object, noting that their First Amendment (free speech) rights are being violated.
6. A secretary on the campus of a tax-supported university has been requested to give her staff password to her supervisor. The supervisor would like to check the secretary's e-mail when she is not at work to see if departmental-related mail is coming in. The secretary is not comfortable giving her password to her supervisor, but is afraid to say no.
7. Tina's e-mail is being diverted and sent out to her entire class. The messages are quite personal and Tina is very embarrassed.
8. Sandy has been receiving four or five anonymous insults daily over e-mail. Because of the context of the notes, she has narrowed the suspect down to someone in her fourth-hour class. She sends the entire class a nasty warning not to do it again.
9. Brad has posted a note on his class newsgroup stating his (highly unflattering) opinion of a new teacher. He wants to know what others think. Some of the responses that follow say nice things. Other comments are quite critical; a few are personal.

From *An Educator's Guide to Information Literacy: What Every High School Senior Needs to Know*. Westport, CT: Libraries Unlimited, 2007. Copyright © 2007 by Ann Marlow Riedling.

10. At Paradise High School, people can send e-mail messages to students-only mailing lists that no teachers or administrators can read. Teachers and administrators also have their own mailing lists. However, word leaks out that the answers to a sophomore-level test have been mailed to the sophomore student mailing list, but no one is saying who is responsible for the posting. Now the school administration is rethinking the idea of student-only areas and the issue of whether the faculty should supervise them.

11. Paula and Ron went out for a few months. During that time, they sent each other some pretty personal e-mail. But their break-up was messy. The final straw came when Ron found out that Paula was sending copies of their old messages to his new girlfriend. Pretty soon, copies of the messages seemed to be all over the school and his new girlfriend wouldn't speak to him.

12. Russ has been an active participant at a chat site for teens. He knows a few of the people in real life, but many live in other cities. One of them, Stuart, will be coming through town in a few weeks and wants to get together. He asks Russ for his home phone number and address. Russ suggests that they just meet at the mall, and Stuart agrees, but wants Russ's home info anyway in case he's delayed.

13. Word gets around that Sylvester maintains a Web site on the Geocities Web server. Besides containing sexually explicit references about a couple of girls at school, the Web site links to hard core porn sites. School officials find out about it and tell Sylvester that they plan to inform his parents about the Web site.

14. Marla figures out that when she is logged into the server she can look at others' directories, make copies of files, and deposit new files. The operating system was designed to allow this functionality so that people could share their work. Mr. Klausinsky objects when he observes Marla poking around in another student's directory. But Marla responds by saying, "If the system allows me to do it and there's no specific rule against it, what's the problem?"

15. After the September 11th terrorist attack, many students and teachers send related e-mail to the all-student or all-faculty mailing lists. Most of the messages contain information about the status of former students and about ways people can help in the crisis. But Penelope sends a long note with a heavy religious message, and Mr. Snidden sends out patriotic graphics and images. A small delegation of students takes their objections to the administration. They understood that these all-school mailing lists, which are screened by the school's system administrator, were supposed to be used for school-related, informational purposes only.

16. Several students have discovered a Web site that promotes anorexia as a lifestyle choice rather than an eating disorder. It includes tips for weight loss, pictures that glamorize the anorexic look, a discussion board members use to support one another, and other material that promotes "anorexic pride." School counselors have asked that this site and others like it be blocked on the school network. They point out that anorexia is a deadly disease and that some students are particularly susceptible to this type of misinformation.

17. Lynn advertises her club fund-raiser by sending out an e-mail to the club's listserv, which has about 500 members. At the bottom of her message, she tells recipients they should reply to the message if they want to be taken off the list. But when recipients e-mail her back, their responses also go to the other 500 people on the list. Many of those people then send replies, asking: "Why did you send me this message? I can't remove you from the list!" Of course, many of these cease and desist messages also go to all 500 members. This e-mailing continues back and forth until people's mailboxes start filling to capacity. New messages start bouncing back to the server, which eventually crashes.

From *An Educator's Guide to Information Literacy: What Every High School Senior Needs to Know.* Westport, CT: Libraries Unlimited, 2007. Copyright © 2007 by Ann Marlow Riedling.

18. Joe uses e-mail/instant messaging/blogging to conduct a popularity poll. He asks "Who are the people you like most in the sophomore class? Who are the people you like least?" A couple of names predominate on the least-liked list. Suzy, who is one of those people, starts missing a lot of school. Her parents are puzzled because the doctor can find nothing physically wrong with her. School officials warn them that Suzy will have to repeat the year if her attendance doesn't improve.

19. Charley, Alfred, and Tim are good friends, but like lots of guys, sometimes get into one-upsmanship games. This time, it started when Charley got himself a new instant messaging screen name no one knew him by. He started messaging people about Alfred, saying things about him that either weren't true or else were pretty private. Finally, Alfred figured out it was Charley who was doing the IMing. So to get back at Charley, Alfred went to a popular Web board and logged on, using Tim's name instead of his own. On this public Web board he posted Charley's real telephone number, saying Charley was a girl looking for a date. When the phone calls started coming in, both Charley and Tim got in trouble.

20. Like many of her friends, Minnie has a blog. But unlike her friends, she keeps its location secret. She doesn't link to anyone else's blog and she doesn't comment on other blogs using her blog identity. Somehow, though, Edward finds out the URL for Minnie's blog and adds it to the "friends" list on his blog. Word spreads, and soon everyone has read Minnie's blog. Unfortunately, she has used her blog to criticize most everyone she knows, including other students, teachers, and her parents. Everyone is furious with her.

21. Some students find a way to obtain system administrator passwords to the school computer network. They learn how to mask the identity of the computers they are logging in from, so no one can trace their actions or figure out who they are. The students use the passwords to poke around the system, including reading and copying some teachers' files and tests. When they finally get caught, they are in big trouble. The students know they have broken the rules, but they claim that they did not delete or change files, look at personal e-mail or student records, or even personally benefit from seeing the tests. Therefore, they feel their punishment should not be too severe.

22. A group of older boys has found out Greg's e-mail address and signed him up for pornographic Web sites. When Greg goes to the library to check his Yahoo e-mail, his inbox is full of "verification" e-mails for these Web sites. Clicking on the "remove" link within these e-mails takes Greg to the sites themselves to unsubscribe—which also brings up detailed graphic images. Ron, one of the reference librarians, sees these images on Greg's screen, which are a violation of the library's Internet policy, and suspends Greg's Internet privileges for one month.

23. The teen librarian has created a group e-mail list for teens so that she can send e-mails publicizing the library's teen programs to them. A teen on the list replies to one of these e-mails with an inappropriate comment about some other teens. Replies flood the e-mail list demanding that this person be suspended from the library.

24. Libby posts some complaints about Mr. Johnson on her MySpace page. She says he's a terrible teacher and that he plays favorites. Roger responds by posting a doctored photo of Mr. Johnson with devil horns and blood coming out of his mouth. Theresa's follow-up comment is that Mr. Johnson "should be fired and put on the police list of sex offenders." More and more people post comments (some with images) until Libby's page comes to the attention of the school administration. Libby and several of the people who posted comments are called in for disciplinary action. The school administration blocks MySpace.com from the school network.

From *An Educator's Guide to Information Literacy: What Every High School Senior Needs to Know*. Westport, CT: Libraries Unlimited, 2007. Copyright © 2007 by Ann Marlow Riedling.

25. Orlando produces a weekly podcast that has become fairly popular in his small town. He broadcasts community news that focuses on teen interests and features regular guest speakers. His listeners especially like the gossip segment of the show, which is written with the help of several unidentified contributors. Lately, he's also been including podcasts of lectures from his history and English classes. Students who miss class appreciate the service, but his teachers are stunned to find out that their lectures are available to anyone who has Internet access.

Intellectual Property Issues

1. Tracy had a report to write on acid rain. She used several sources—books, magazines, newspaper articles, and an electronic encyclopedia. She listed all these sources in her bibliography at the end of the report. She found the encyclopedia to be the most convenient source because she could highlight portions of the text and paste them into her word processing document.
2. Jason R. designed and posted a Star Wars Web site. Once the site started receiving 40,000 hits a day, he received a phone call from Lucasfilm asking him to shut it down. Jason posted excerpts of the phone conversation on his Web site. Lucasfilm was then flooded with angry e-mail messages from fans who felt the company was exerting totalitarian control over products to which they felt a deep personal connection.
3. Ms. Harris received e-mail from someone who liked the gargoyle image on the Uni High Library's Web page and wanted to know if he could use it on his school library's Web page. The art teacher, who created the image for the school, wrote back to him, explaining that the image belonged to the university and that, furthermore, it had special significance as the image that identifies Uni High. She thanked him for his interest, but told him that she could not grant permission for him to use it.
4. Richard asked Vicky if he could look at the essay she wrote for their history class. She told him "sure" and thought no more about it. Several days after the essays were turned in, the teacher asked her to stay after class. She showed Vicky that her essay and Richard's were almost identical. She asked Vicky for an explanation.
5. Malcolm has a Web page on the topic of sailboats. He has collected a truly astonishing amount of information and receives many complimentary e-mail messages from sailing enthusiasts. He has downloaded numerous pictures and articles he finds on other Web sites, and is always careful to give credit by citing the original sources.
6. Paramount Pictures has cracked down on numerous Star Trek fans for printing synopses of the plots of just-released installments in the film series. In other media news, Fox TV sent a cease and desist letter to a woman whose Simpsons icons were starting to appear across various Web sites. She is quoted as saying that she felt she was giving Fox free publicity.
7. Roberta and Todd are the DJs for the next school dance. They surf the Web for their favorite MP3s and download several songs, which they burn onto a CD to play at the dance. Some of the songs are from big name groups and others are from new artists who are using the Web to build an audience.
8. Mr. Boxley asks the school librarian to check some references in Belinda's research paper. Mr. Boxley believes that the writing is far better than Belinda's usual work, almost spookily better. The librarian does a quick search and discovers that Belinda has copied whole paragraphs from the online articles she cites. However, in each sentence, at least two words have been changed. When confronted, Belinda argues that she has paraphrased and cited her sources. She does not believe she has plagiarized from other people's work.

9. Larry is a fan of a superheroes cartoon that has an accompanying Web site. He particularly likes one of the characters. He copies the character's Web page onto his own Web page, but changes the name of the character to "Larry." Several weeks later, the school system administrator is contacted by the company that produces the show and the Web page. They threaten to sue the school if the site is not immediately removed.

10. Ken really enjoys music but doesn't have much money to buy new CDs. He notices that the public library has a lot of CDs and decides to check them out. Once Ken has the CDs at home he realizes that he can burn the CDs and keep copies for himself.

11. Mun-Hwa has a paper due second period but doesn't do any work until the night before. She heads to the public library where she asks the librarians for help. After they've shown her how to e-mail documents from online databases to her home, Mun-Hwa realizes that she can easily cut and paste paragraphs from the articles she retrieved into a document without citing them and that her teachers would never know.

Puzzle: Which scenario in the first list also belongs in the second list under Intellectual Property Issues?

Library Staff Ethics Issues

1. The teen librarian wants to create a group e-mail list for teens so that she can send e-mail publicizing the library's teen programs to them. She runs a query on the patron database and extracts e-mail addresses for anyone born between the appropriate years so she can be sure to inform as many teens as possible about the great programs at the library.

2. After the September 11th terrorist attack, many library staff send related e-mail to the all-youth, all-reference, or all-staff mailing lists. Most of the messages contain information about the status of former patrons and friends of the library and about ways people can help in the crisis. But Penelope, a circulation clerk, sends a long note with a heavy religions message, and Dave, a library assistant, sends out patriotic graphics and images. A small delegation of library staff takes their objections to the administration. They understood that these library mailing lists were supposed to be used for library-related, informational purposes only.

3. The library secretary has been requested to give her computer password to the library director. The director would like to check her e-mail when she is not at work to see if library-related mail is coming in. The secretary is not comfortable giving her password to her director, but is afraid to say no.

Reprinted by permission, Frances Jacobson Harris, University Laboratory High School, University of Illinois at Urbana-Champaign.

From *An Educator's Guide to Information Literacy: What Every High School Senior Needs to Know*. Westport, CT: Libraries Unlimited, 2007. Copyright © 2007 by Ann Marlow Riedling.

Lesson 3.38: Works Cited Information

NAME: _____ DATE: _____

For this lesson, create a Works Cited page with materials you have located for your research topic.

Works Cited

Barker, Karen. *Women of Steel*. New York: Knopf, 1991.

Brown, Charlie. "My Life in Cartoons." *Cartoon Week* 21 Nov. 1999:7–12. *InfoTrac: General Reference Center Gold*. Gale Group. 15 Dec. 1999. <http://galenet.gale.com>

Evans, Harold. "Coping With Unruly Children." *Time* 15 Feb. 1994: 25–29.

———. "Bringing Up Billy." *Newsweek* 17 June 2000: 31–33.

Goldsmith, Elizabeth. "The Future is Dim." *Fresno Bee* 5 July 1996: 3A

Dakota. 24 June 2002. <www.usa.coldwar.server.gov/index/coldwar.html>

Moyers, Bill, dir. *Maya Angelou*. PBS Home Video, New York, 1991.

Pasquier, Roger F. "Owl." *Encyclopedia Americana Online*. Grolier, Inc., 2002. 29 Feb. 2002. <http://ea.grolier.com>

Works Cited List Format

- Begin your works cited list on a separate page from the text of the essay under the label Works Cited (with no quotation marks, underlining, etc.), which should be centered at the top of the page.
- Make the first line of each entry in your list flush left with the margin. Subsequent lines in each entry should be indented one-half inch. This is known as a hanging indent.
- Single space between lines of an entry. Double space between one entry and another.
- Keep in mind that underlining and *italics* are equivalent; you should select one or the other to use throughout your essay.
- Alphabetize the list of works cited by the first word in each entry (usually the author's last name).

Basic Rules for Citations

- Authors' names are inverted (last name first); if a work has more than one author, invert only the first author's name, follow it with a comma, then continue listing the rest of the authors.
- If you have cited more than one work by a particular author, order them alphabetically by title, and use three hyphens in place of the author's name for every entry after the first.
- When an author appears both as the sole author of a text and as the first author of a group, list sole-author entries first.
- If no author is given for a particular work, alphabetize by the title of the piece and use a shortened version of the title for parenthetical citations.

- Capitalize each word in the titles of articles, books, etc. This rule does not apply to articles, short prepositions, or conjunctions unless one is the first word of the title or subtitle.
- Underline or italicize titles of books, journals, magazines, newspapers, and films.
- Use quotation marks around the titles of articles in journals, magazines, and newspapers. Also use quotation marks for the titles of short stories, book chapters, poems, and songs.
- List page numbers efficiently, when needed. If you refer to a journal article that appeared on pages 225 through 250, list the page numbers on your Works Cited page as 225–50.
- If you're citing an article or a publication that was originally issued in print form but that you retrieved from an online database, you should provide enough information so that the reader can locate the article either in its original print form or retrieve it from the online database (if they have access).

Lesson 3.39: Works Cited

NAME: _____ DATE: _____

For this lesson, fill in the blanks for all types of resources.

WORKS CITED INFORMATION

BOOKS

Author: _____

Title: _____

City of publication: _____

Publishing co.:_____

Copyright date: _____

How to put it all together on your final works cited list:

Lastname, Firstname. *Title Of The Book Italicized*. City: Publisher, Date.

WORKS CITED INFORMATION

GENERAL ENCYCLOPEDIAS

Author of *article* (if there is one): _____

Title of *article:* _____

Title of *encyclopedia:* _____

Copyright date ed: _____ (example: 2002 ed.)

How to put it all together on your final works cited list:

Lastname, Firstname. "Title of Article in Quotes." *Title of Encyclopedia italicized*. Year ed.

WORKS CITED INFORMATION

REFERENCE BOOKS

Author of *article* (if there is one): _____

Title of *article:* _____

Title of *reference book or series :* _____

Editor or author of the reference book/series (if there is one): _____

Number of volumes in the set: _____ (example: 5 vols.)

City of publication: _____

Publishing co.: _____

Copyright date: _____

How to put it all together on your final works cited list:

Lastname, Firstname. "Title of Article in Quotes." *Title of Reference Book Italicized.* Editor's Firstname Lastname, ed. #vols. City of publication: Publishing company, year.

WORKS CITED INFORMATION

ONLINE ENCYCLOPEDIAS

Author of *article:* _____

Title of *article:* _____

Title of *Encyc.* (*Americana, Grolier,* or *New Book of Knowledge*): _____

Title of the *Database or Online Service:* _____

Copyright date: _____

Date of access (date you printed the article): _____

Web address of online service: _____

How to put it all together on your final works cited list:

Lastname, Firstname. "Title Of The Article In Quotes." *Title of Encyclopedia.* Publisher, copyright date. Date of access. <http://address/filename>

Note: Dates should be typed in the following format: 12 November 2002.

WORKS CITED INFORMATION

ONLINE DATABASES

(For example: InfoTrac)

Format for a periodical reference (newspaper, magazine or journal)

Author of *article:* _____

Title of *article:* _____

Original source (Name of *periodical*): _____

Date of periodical: _____

Page range **OR** total number of pages of the article (if available): _____

Title of *Online Database:* _____

Publisher: _____

Date of access (date you printed the article): _____

Database home page address: _____

How to put it all together on your final works cited list:

Lastname, Firstname. "Title Of The Article In Quotes." *Title of Periodical* Date: page range. Title of Online Database. Publisher. Date of Access. <http://galenet.gale.com>

Note: Dates should be typed in the following format: 12 November 2002.

From *An Educator's Guide to Information Literacy: What Every High School Senior Needs to Know.* Westport, CT: Libraries Unlimited, 2007. Copyright © 2007 by Ann Marlow Riedling.

WORKS CITED INFORMATION

INTERNET WEB PAGES

Author (if known): _____

Title of page or document: _____

Title of site or larger work: _____

Date document was written/updated/posted: _____

Name of any associated institution: _____

Date of access (date you printed the article): _____

URL (address) of document: _____

How to put it all together on your final works cited list:

Lastname, Firstname. "Title Of The Web Page In Quotes." *Title of Site or Larger Work Italicized.* Date Written. Name of any Associated Institution. Date of access <http://www.website.org/page.htm>

Note: Dates should be typed in the following format: 12 November 2002.

From Works Cited lessons found on the Gananda High School Library Web site. http://www.gananda.k12.ny.us/library/mshslibrary/evalunit.htm

WORKS CITED INFORMATION

MAGAZINE/PERIODICAL ARTICLES (PRINT)

Author: _____

Title of article: _____

Title of magazine: _____

Date: _____

Pages: _____

How to put it all together on your final works cited list:

Lastname, Firstname. *Title of the magazine italicized.* Day month year: pages.

NEWSPAPER ARTICLE (PRINT)

Author: _____

Title of article: _____

Name of newspaper: _____

Date: _____

Page and section: _____

How to put it all together on your final works cited list:

Lastname, Firstname. *Name of newspaper italicized.* day month year: page and section.

Permission granted by Purdue University, OWL Writing Lab, 2006.

From *An Educator's Guide to Information Literacy: What Every High School Senior Needs to Know.* Westport, CT: Libraries Unlimited, 2007. Copyright © 2007 by Ann Marlow Riedling.

Lesson 3.40: Chicago Manual of Style

NAME: _____ DATE: _____

Read the following information regarding *Chicago Manual of Style* documentation on this Web site: http://www.chicagomanualofstyle.org/tools.html.

Now practice using this style by citing the following (your choice of materials to use):

1. Book with one author
2. Book with two authors
3. Book with three or more authors
4. Editor, translator, or compiler
5. Chapter or other part of a book
6. Preface, foreword, introduction, and similar parts of a book
7. Books published in both printed and electronic forms
8. Journal article
9. Popular magazine article
10. Newspaper article
11. Theses/dissertations
12. Paper presented at a meeting or conference
13. Personal communications

From *An Educator's Guide to Information Literacy: What Every High School Senior Needs to Know*. Westport, CT: Libraries Unlimited, 2007. Copyright © 2007 by Ann Marlow Riedling.

4

Checklists for Each ACRL Standard

The following checklists are for both the student and instructor. They are provided to supply a monitor of information literacy skills assessments—check off lists to streamline the process of understanding information literacy. Checklists are divided into sections according to the ACRL standards. These checklists may be copied as handouts (for instructors) or study sheets (for students).

Checklists for Standard 1

The information literate student determines the nature and extent of the information needed.

Checklists for Standard 1

NAME: _____ DATE: _____

The information literate student will:

1. Participate in class discussions _____
2. Consult with instructors _____
3. Participate in peer workgroups _____
4. Participate in electronic discussions _____
5. Develop a thesis statement _____
6. Formulate questions based on the information need _____

NAME: _____ DATE: _____

The information literate student:

1. Knows how information is produced _____
2. Knows how information is organized _____
3. Knows how information is disseminated _____
4. Recognizes that knowledge can be organized into disciplines _____
5. Identifies the value of potential resources in a variety of formats _____
6. Identifies the differences of potential resources in a variety of formats _____
7. Identifies the purpose of potential resources _____
8. Identifies the audience of potential resources _____
9. Differentiates between primary and secondary sources _____
10. Recognizes that primary and secondary sources vary with each discipline _____
11. Realizes that information may need to be constructed with raw data _____

NAME: _____ DATE: _____

The information literate student:

1. Determines the availability of needed information   _____

2. Makes decisions on broadening the information-seeking process   _____

3. Considers the feasibility of acquiring a new language or skill   _____

4. Defines a realistic overall plan to acquire needed information   _____

5. Defines a realistic overall timeline to acquire needed information   _____

NAME: _____ DATE: _____

The information literate student:

1. Reviews the initial information need to clarify the question   _____

2. Reviews the initial information need to revise the question   _____

3. Reviews the initial information need to refine the question   _____

4. Describes criteria used to make information decisions   _____

5. Describes criteria used to make information choices   _____

From *An Educator's Guide to Information Literacy: What Every High School Senior Needs to Know*. Westport, CT: Libraries Unlimited, 2007. Copyright © 2007 by Ann Marlow Riedling.

Checklists for Standard 2

The information literate student accesses needed information effectively and efficiently.

Checklists for Standard 2

NAME: _____ DATE: _____

The information literate student:

1. Identifies appropriate investigative methods   _____
2. Investigates benefits of various investigative methods   _____
3. Investigates applicability of various investigative methods   _____
4. Investigates the scope of information retrieval systems   _____
5. Investigates the content of information retrieval systems   _____
6. Investigates the organization of information retrieval systems   _____
7. Selects efficient approaches for accessing needed information   _____
8. Selects effective approaches for accessing needed information   _____

NAME: _____ DATE: _____

The information literate student:

1. Develops a research plan appropriate to the investigative method   _____
2. Identifies keywords for the information needed   _____
3. Identifies synonyms for the information needed   _____
4. Identifies related terms for the information needed   _____
5. Selects controlled vocabulary specific to the discipline   _____
6. Selects controlled vocabulary specific to the information retrieval source   _____
7. Constructs a search strategy using appropriate commands for the system   _____
8. Implements the search strategy using different user interfaces   _____
9. Implements the search strategy using different search engines   _____
10. Implements the search strategy with different command languages   _____
11. Implements the search strategy with different protocols   _____
12. Implements the search strategy with different search parameters   _____
13. Implements the search using appropriate investigative protocols   _____

NAME: _____ DATE: _____

The information literate student:

1. Uses various search systems to retrieve information in a variety of formats _____
2. Uses various classification schemes to locate information sources _____
3. Uses specialized online services to retrieve information needed _____
4. Uses specialized in-person services to retrieve information needed _____
5. Uses surveys to retrieve primary information _____
6. Uses letters to retrieve primary information _____
7. Uses interviews to retrieve primary information _____

NAME: _____ DATE: _____

The information literate student:

1. Assesses the quantity of the search results _____
2. Assesses the quality of the search results _____
3. Assesses the relevance of the search results _____
4. Identifies gaps in the information retrieved for possible revisions _____
5. Repeats the search using revised strategy as necessary _____

NAME: _____ DATE: _____

The information literate student:

1. Selects among various technologies the most appropriate one _____
2. Creates a system for organizing the information _____
3. Differentiates between the types of sources cited _____
4. Understands the elements and correct syntax of a citation _____
5. Records all pertinent citation information for future reference _____
6. Uses various technologies to manage the information selected _____

From *An Educator's Guide to Information Literacy: What Every High School Senior Needs to Know*. Westport, CT: Libraries Unlimited, 2007. Copyright © 2007 by Ann Marlow Riedling.

Checklists for Standard 3

The information literate student evaluates information and its sources critically and incorporates selected information into his or her knowledge base and value system.

Checklists for Standard 3

NAME: _____ DATE: _____

The information literate student:

1. Reads the text and selects main ideas _____
2. Restates textual concepts in his or her own words _____
3. Selects data accurately _____
4. Identifies verbatim material that can be appropriately quoted _____

NAME: _____ DATE: _____

The information literate student:

1. Examines and compares information in order to evaluate reliability _____
2. Examines and compares information in order to evaluate validity _____
3. Examines and compares information in order to evaluate accuracy _____
4. Examines and compares information in order to evaluate authority _____
5. Examines and compares information in order to evaluate timeliness _____
6. Examines and compares information in order to evaluate bias _____
7. Analyzes the structure and logic of supporting arguments or methods _____
8. Recognizes prejudice, deception, or manipulation _____
9. Recognizes the cultural context within which the information was created _____
10. Recognizes the physical context within which the information was created _____
11. Understands the impact of context on interpreting the information _____

NAME: _____ DATE: _____

The information literate student:

1. Recognizes interrelationships among concepts _____
2. Combines concepts into potentially useful statements with evidence _____
3. Extends initial synthesis at a higher level to construct new hypotheses _____
4. Utilizes technologies for studying the interaction of ideas _____

From *An Educator's Guide to Information Literacy: What Every High School Senior Needs to Know*. Westport, CT: Libraries Unlimited, 2007. Copyright © 2007 by Ann Marlow Riedling.

NAME: _____ DATE: _____

The information literate student:

1. Determines whether information satisfies the research   _____
2. Uses selected criteria to determine contradictions from other sources   _____
3. Uses selected criteria to determine verification from other sources   _____
4. Draws conclusions based upon information gathered   _____
5. Tests theories with discipline-appropriate techniques   _____
6. Determines probable accuracy by questioning the source of data   _____
7. Determines probable accuracy by noting limitations of the tools   _____
8. Determines probable accuracy by noting the reasonableness of conclusions   _____
9. Integrates new information with previous information or knowledge   _____
10. Selects information that provides evidence for the topic   _____

NAME: _____ DATE: _____

The information literate student:

1. Investigates differing viewpoints encountered in the literature   _____
2. Determines whether to incorporate or reject viewpoints encountered   _____
3. Participates in classroom and other discussions   _____
4. Participates in class-sponsored electronic communication forums   _____
5. Seeks expert opinion through a variety of mechanisms   _____

NAME: _____ DATE: _____

The information literate student:

1. Determines if the original information need has been satisfied   _____
2. Determines if the original information need requires more information   _____
3. Reviews the search strategy and incorporates additional concepts   _____
4. Reviews information retrieval sources used and uses more if necessary   _____

Checklists for Standard 4

The information literate student, individually or as a member of a group, uses information effectively to accomplish a specific purpose.

Checklists for Standard 4

NAME: _____ DATE: _____

The information literate student:

1. Organizes the content in a manner that supports the purposes _____
2. Organizes the content in a manner that supports the format _____
3. Articulates knowledge and skills transferred from prior experiences _____
4. Integrates new and prior information to support the purposes _____
5. Manipulates digital text, as needed _____
6. Manipulates images, as needed _____
7. Displays data, as needed _____

NAME: _____ DATE: _____

The information literate student:

1. Maintains a journal of activities related to information seeking _____
2. Maintains a journal of activities related to evaluating information _____
3. Maintains a journal of activities related to the communicating process _____
4. Reflects on past successes, failures, and alternative strategies _____
5. Chooses a communication medium that supports the purposes _____
6. Chooses a communication format that supports the purposes _____
7. Uses a range of technologies in creating a product _____
8. Incorporates principles of design and communication _____
9. Communicates clearly and with a style that supports the audience _____

From *An Educator's Guide to Information Literacy: What Every High School Senior Needs to Know*. Westport, CT: Libraries Unlimited, 2007. Copyright © 2007 by Ann Marlow Riedling.

Checklists for Standard 5

The information literate student understands many of the ethical, legal, and socio-economic issues surrounding the use of information and accesses and uses information ethically and legally.

Checklists for Standard 5

NAME: _____ DATE: _____

The information literate student:

1. Identifies and discusses issues related to privacy and security   _____

2. Identifies and discusses issues related to free and fee-based access   _____

3. Identifies and discusses issues related to censorship   _____

4. Identifies and discusses issues related to freedom of speech   _____

5. Demonstrates an understanding of intellectual property   _____

6. Demonstrates an understanding of copyright   _____

7. Demonstrates an understanding of fair use   _____

NAME: _____ DATE: _____

The information literate student:

1. Participates in electronic discussions following accepted practices   _____

2. Uses approved passwords for access to information resources   _____

3. Complies with institutional policies on access to resources   _____

4. Preserves the integrity of information resources   _____

5. Preserves the integrity of information equipment   _____

6. Preserves the integrity of information systems   _____

7. Preserves the integrity of information facilities   _____

8. Legally obtains, stores, and disseminates text, data, images, and sounds   _____

9. Demonstrates an understanding of plagiarism   _____

10. Does not plagiarize   _____

11. Understands institutional policies related to human subjects research   _____

12. Selects an appropriate documentation style for citing sources   _____

13. Posts permission-granted notices for copyrighted material   _____

From *An Educator's Guide to Information Literacy: What Every High School Senior Needs to Know*. Westport, CT: Libraries Unlimited, 2007. Copyright © 2007 by Ann Marlow Riedling.

5

Formative Assessments for Each ACRL Standard

How can you assess information literacy? Should you assess the process or the product? Should there be an information literacy graduation requirement? Media specialists and educators often ponder these questions and others connected with the implementation of information literacy programs.

This chapter offers a variety of formative assessments and rubrics for each ACRL information literacy standard. Obviously, these are merely a few possibilities—with your creativity and imagination, I am certain you will discover even more and different ones. Information literacy is not easily assessed; therefore, careful consideration of each student and each assignment should be made.

Formative Assessments for Standard 1

The information literate student determines the nature and extent of the information needed.

Assessment 1.1
(Teacher Assessment of Students)

Students visit a library to conduct their own research. Appropriate library staff serve as guides to assist students as they pursue their topics. Students hand in research results at the end of the class session, including:

- copies of articles
- computer printouts of search results
- worksheets provided by their teacher
- other necessary data

Checklist

Articles	Superb choices = 3	Good choices = 2	Needs Improvement = 1	Total =
Printouts	Superb choices = 3	Good choices = 2	Needs Improvement = 1	Total =
Worksheets	Superb choices = 3	Good choices = 2	Needs Improvement = 1	Total =
Other Data	Superb choices = 3	Good choices = 2	Needs Improvement = 1	Total =

Assessment 1.2
(Teacher Assessment of Students)

Students write a proposal describing a research paper. They do research for the paper but do not actually write the paper. The proposal must include:

- thesis statement
- questions to be answered by the research
- sources consulted (number, quality, appropriateness)
- bibliography of resources in APA format

Checklist

Thesis Statement	Superior = 3	Good = 2	Needs Improvement = 1	Total =
Questions	Superior = 3	Good = 2	Needs Improvement = 1	Total =
Sources	Superior = 3	Good = 2	Needs Improvement = 1	Total =
Bibliography	Superior = 3	Good = 2	Needs Improvement = 1	Total =

From *An Educator's Guide to Information Literacy: What Every High School Senior Needs to Know.* Westport, CT: Libraries Unlimited, 2007. Copyright © 2007 by Ann Marlow Riedling.

Assessment 1.3
(Teacher Assessment of Students)

Research Portfolio

The portfolio must include:

- lists of articles, book chapters, or other resources the student found most useful for his or her research
- a brief description of why the student felt the item was useful

Checklist

Resources	Superior=3	Good=2	Needs Improvement=1	Total=
Description	Superior=3	Good=2	Needs Improvement=1	Total=

Assessment 1.4
(Teacher Assessment of Students)

Research Worksheet

- Students create a printed worksheet that guides them through research in one or more resources, such as catalogs, journal indexes, reference books, and so forth.
- The worksheet provides instructions for using the source(s) and includes space for writing about what was found in that source.

Students may choose their own topics or the topics may have been assigned.

When the worksheet is completed, it will include:

- key words and subject headings that led to useful information in the source
- citations found (number and appropriateness)
- location of the materials used (worksheet provided by the instructor)
- evaluation of the source's usefulness for the project
- one or more bibliographic citations in APA format

Checklist

Key words/Subject Headings	Superior = 3	Good = 2	Needs Improvement = 1	Total =
Citations Found	Superior = 3	Good = 2	Needs Improvement = 1	Total =
Location Used	Superior = 3	Good = 2	Needs Improvement = 1	Total =
Evaluation Useful	Superior = 3	Good = 2	Needs Improvement = 1	Total =
Bibliographic Citations	Superior = 3	Good = 2	Needs Improvement = 1	Total =

Assessment 1.5
(Teacher Assessment of Students)

Scholarly Journals vs. Popular Magazine Articles: Please list the following characteristics as they appear for scholarly journals and popular magazines.

Characteristics	Scholarly Journals	Popular Magazines
How can you tell the difference between these types of articles?		
What is the difference in length?		
What are the differences in language/audience?		
How do the format and structure of each vary?		
Who are the editors for each?		

Assessment 1.6
(Teacher Assessment of Students)

You are a researcher—for a class project. Discuss the following issues related to effective and efficient research: questioning, gathering, planning, sorting, synthesizing, evaluating, and reporting.

Checklists:

Questioning: A researcher uses appropriate, accurate, timely, and thought-provoking questioning techniques.

Discovers independently an issue or problem that needs a solution after exploring the topic = 3

Formulates questions about topics with adult help to elevate the question to focus on issues = 2

Relies upon adults to state questions and topics = 1

Planning: A researcher identifies sources of information likely to build understanding.

Selects high quality sources independently and efficiently = 3

Selects sources with mixed success = 2

Wanders from source to source without questioning which source will be most helpful = 1

Gathering: A researcher collects and stores information for later consideration.

Collects and organizes important information for retrieval independently = 3

Collects information with some degree of organization = 2

Loses track of most important information = 1

Sorting: A researcher reorganizes information so that the most valuable becomes readily available to support understanding.

Creates structure that provides a coherent and clear focus = 3

Creates partial organization of information = 2

Leaves information as gathered = 1

Synthesizing: A researcher recombines information to develop decisions and solutions.

Creates an original decision or solution = 3

Recognizes and combines strategies of others = 2

Restates the decisions and solutions of others = 1

Evaluating: A researcher determines whether the information gathered is sufficient to support a conclusion.

Tests solutions and decisions to see if supporting information is adequate = 3

Looks for missing information = 2

Reaches a hasty conclusion = 1

Reporting: A researcher translates findings into a persuasive, instructive, or effective product(s).

  Creates and presents an original product that effectively addresses original problem or
      issues = 3
  Provides a product that offers some insight with regard to the original problem or
      issues = 2
  Shares the work or thoughts of others = 1

Assessment 1.7
(Student Self Assessment)

Checklist: Information literacy skills using secondary sources

I understand research models. I understand and effectively use secondary sources. I use and cite electronic information sources. I use computer productivity software. I use technology and share the results of my research with others. I reinforce information literacy skills on a daily basis as opportunities arise = 3

I have library research projects and I support the library skills taught. I am familiar with secondary sources and am aware that there are electronic resources available for my use = 2

I am not familiar with the terms *information literacy* or *secondary sources,* nor do I know why such skills are important = 1

Checklist: Information literacy skills using primary sources

I collect original data to answer genuine questions. I may use tools to collect data like computerized probes and sensors, online surveys, interviews, or digitized sources of historical records, as well as tools to record, organize, and communicate the data such databases and spreadsheets = 3

I collect and use original data. I generally can predict the outcome of such experiments = 2

I only use secondary resources like books, magazines, or reference materials = 1

Checklist: Newsgroups and electronic mailing lists

I read the newsgroups that interest me on a regular basis, and I can contribute to newsgroups. I can subscribe, unsubscribe, and contribute to electronic mailing lists (listservs) related to my research. I know how to find, configure, and use the specialized tools for newsgroups and mailing lists. I can access and search mailing list archives = 3

I know that there are resources in a variety of formats available on the Internet, but cannot confidently access them = 2

I have no knowledge of newsgroups or electronic mailing list functions = 1

From *An Educator's Guide to Information Literacy: What Every High School Senior Needs to Know.* Westport, CT: Libraries Unlimited, 2007. Copyright © 2007 by Ann Marlow Riedling.

Assessment 1.8
(Teacher Assessment of Students)

Quiz

1. The best place to look for an introduction to a topic such as astronomy is:

   a) the online catalog   b) an encyclopedia   c) a periodical   d) none of these

2. "Describe the effects of a thinning ozone layer on the environment." What are the key concepts in this statement?

   a) effect, environment   b) environment, ozone layer   c) effects, thinning

3. What source would best answer the question?

   a) dictionary   b) map   c) periodical index   d) directory

4. "Discuss how the breakup of the Soviet Union has improved U.S. foreign policy." What are the key concepts?

   a) breakup, foreign policy, U.S., Soviet Union   b) Soviet Union, U.S.   c) U.S., foreign policy, Soviet Union

5. "Discuss capital punishment as a deterrent to crime." Which of the following statements will get the best information from a database search?

   a) capital punishment or crime   b) deterrent and crime
   c) capital punishment and crime

6. "Describe the characteristics of an asthma or hay fever attack." Which of the following search statements will obtain the best results from a database search?

   a) asthma and hay fever   b) asthma or hay fever   c) characteristics and attack

7. You can use the library's online catalog to find information on:

   a) all books published in Kentucky   b) University of Louisville's faculty and courses
   c) books for sale   d) books and journal titles owned by the library

8. A periodical index is used to:

   a) locate journal articles   b) find video titles   c) look for books   d) none of these

9. A bibliography is a list of:

   a) addresses   b) phone numbers   c) information sources   d) corporations

10. To find the most current information on your topic, you would consult:

    a) books   b) periodical articles   c) encyclopedia articles   d) bibliographies

From *An Educator's Guide to Information Literacy: What Every High School Senior Needs to Know*. Westport, CT: Libraries Unlimited, 2007. Copyright © 2007 by Ann Marlow Riedling.

11. You consult a dictionary to find information on:

   a) titles owned by the library   b) meanings of words
   c) articles on a topic   d) addresses

12. Which of the following oral presentation topics requires the most current information?

   a) critique of Maya Angelou's poem "On the Pulse of Morning"
   b) effects of global warming on climate
   c) issues in Zimbabwe's push for independence
   d) reaction to India's nuclear weapon tests

Examine the following Web page and answer the questions: http://www.d-b.net/dti.

13. Is there an indication of when the information was created or updated?

   a) yes   b) no   c) cannot tell

14. Is there information about the author or creator of the Web site?

   a) yes   b) no   c) cannot tell

15. Is there contact information (for example, e-mail address)?
   a) yes   b) no   c) cannot tell

16. Does the Web site cover the topic extensively?

   a) yes   b) no   c) cannot tell

17. Is the information presented as fact (vs. opinion)?

   a) yes   b) no   c) cannot tell

18. When performing a search with a search engine such as Google, which search statement will find fewer items?

   a) blue and red   b) blue or red   c) they will find the same number

19. Which of the following is the best description of the Internet?

   a) a big computer somewhere that contains a large amount of information
   b) a collection of interconnected big computers managed by universities, the government, and large organizations
   c) a huge number of computers of various sizes that are connected to each other and that can belong to anyone

Assessment 1.9
(Student Self Assessment)

Checklist: Responsible Use

I understand and follow school rules concerning harassment, language, passwords, privacy, copyright, appropriate use and citation of resources, etc. = 3

I take care of the equipment I use and leave it in ready condition for the next user = 2

I do not understand what responsible use means = 1

Checklist: Basic Computer Use

I learn new programs and discover additional program features on my own = 4

I open programs from icons and the Start Bar, and I use more than one program = 3

I log on, log off, open, use, and close programs on my own = 2

I learn new programs and discover additional program features on my own = 1

Checklist: File Management

I use the district network effectively by moving between drives and maintaining my hard drive within network limits = 4

I create my own folders to keep files organized and know how to identify the date and size of each file and folder = 3

I select, open, and save documents on different drives = 2

I do not save any documents I create using the computer = 1

Checklist: E-mail

I use e-mail to request or send information for research or school projects = 4

I organize my mail folders to save messages and delete those I no longer need = 3

I compose and send appropriate e-mail messages and delete those I no longer need = 2

I do not use e-mail = 1

Checklist: Word Processing

I use word processing tools to edit, compare, or improve my previous drafts and publish a final document = 4

I use word processing tools (font style, spell check, grammar check) to edit my work = 3

I use a word processor for basic writing tasks = 2

I do not use a word processor = 1

Checklist: Graphics

I select and modify graphics (example: digital photos, scanned drawings) in order to make a point or illustrate what I have learned = 4

I insert my own graphics and clip art, citing my sources = 3

I create pictures with painting and drawing programs = 2

I do not use graphics = 1

Checklist: Desktop Publishing

I design original publications that communicate to others what I have learned = 4

I create original publications from a blank page, combining design elements such as columns, clip art, tables, word art, and captions = 3

I use templates or wizards to create a published document = 2

I do not use a publishing program = 1

Checklist: Spreadsheet

I use spreadsheets to analyze information, solve problems, and complete assignments = 4

I use graphs and charts to communicate the meaning of my information = 3

I design, create, modify, and troubleshoot spreadsheets = 2

I do not use a spreadsheet = 1

Checklist: Library Database

I use hyperlinks in the library database to find related topics or titles in the library = 4

I use the information in the library database to locate and select books for research or reading = 3

I search for books and videotapes in the library using Title, Author, Subject, and Key word files = 2

I do not use library catalog databases = 1

Checklist: Research/Information Searching

I analyze, evaluate, and communicate the information I've gathered, and credit the sources I have used = 4

I select, gather, and use information from multiple electronic sources to answer a question = 3

I locate information in electronic sources = 2

I do not use electronic sources to find information = 1

Checklist: Internet

I evaluate and select Internet information that is reliable, accurate, and appropriate to my research question = 4

I use various search engines to efficiently locate information on my research question = 3

I visit school-selected Web sites and use navigation buttons to move between pages = 2

I do not use the Internet = 1

Checklist: Technology Presentation

I create original presentations that are well organized and use them to effectively share information or persuade an audience = 4

I start with a blank presentation, and then add text, pictures, and sound to create original presentations = 3

I use templates to create technology presentations = 2

I do not use technology for presentations = 1

From *An Educator's Guide to Information Literacy: What Every High School Senior Needs to Know*. Westport, CT: Libraries Unlimited, 2007. Copyright © 2007 by Ann Marlow Riedling.

Assessment 1.10
(Teacher Assessment of Students)

An individual who operates at the basic level of information literacy:

…appreciates the richness and complexity of the information environment. He or she can describe the wide array of information sources available and discuss their appropriateness for a given information problem.

Possible Measurement Techniques:

- Essay examination
- Oral report
- Practicum in the library
- Written evaluation assignment

…when given an information problem, will be able to conduct a search of multiple information sources within a limited period of time.

Possible Measurement Techniques

- Essay examination
- Pathfinder assignment
- Practical problem to solve

…recognizes the need for information to solve a specific problem and knows what kind of information to seek; is able to refine it and formulate a research question.

Possible Measurement Techniques

- Collaborative learning exercise in class
- Essay examination
- Practical problem to solve

…when given specific problems or problem questions, is be able to identify which ones require information in order to solve the problem.

Possible Measurement Techniques

- Collaborative learning exercise in class
- Essay examination
- Multiple choice examination
- Practical problem to solve

…is able to define the broad categories of information sources, such reference books, journals, or Internet resources.

Possible Measurement Techniques

- Collaborative learning exercise in class
- Multiple choice examination
- Practical problem to solve
- Short answer examination

From *An Educator's Guide to Information Literacy: What Every High School Senior Needs to Know*. Westport, CT: Libraries Unlimited, 2007. Copyright © 2007 by Ann Marlow Riedling.

…will be able to define the broad categories of finding tools, such as periodical indexes or online catalogs.

Possible Measurement Techniques
- Collaborative learning exercise in class
- Multiple choice examination
- Practical problem to solve
- Short answer examination

…will be able to describe the characteristics of types of information sources, such as books and journals.

Possible Measurement Techniques
- Essay examination
- Multiple choice examination
- Short answer examination

…generally understands how knowledge is organized, stored, and transmitted, and is able to describe the principles of the classification systems used to organize information in libraries.

Possible Measurement Techniques
- Essay examination
- Multiple choice examination
- Short answer examination

Possible Measurement Techniques
- Bibliography accompanying paper or speech
- Collaborative learning exercise in class
- Critique of a classmate's completed search/bibliography
- Pathfinder assignment
- Practical problem to solve
- Research paper proposal

…will be able to define the role of controlled vocabulary in systems used to provide access to information.

Possible Measurement Techniques
- Essay examination with a practical problem to solve
- Short answer examination

…will be able to analyze search results from key word searching and subject searching.

Possible Measurement Techniques
- Annotated bibliography with search strategy discussion included
- Essay examination with a sample search
- Paper and pencil exercise with sample search, in class or as homework
- Research journal
- Research portfolio

…will be able to discuss the relationship of citations to other information sources.

Possible Measurement Techniques
- Annotated bibliography with search strategy discussion included
- Essay examination
- Research journal
- Research portfolio

…will be able to discuss appropriate unrecorded information sources and evaluate their potential usefulness.

Possible Measurement Techniques
- Annotated bibliography with search strategy discussion included
- Essay examination
- Research journal
- Research portfolio
- Research paper proposal

…will be able to describe and execute an appropriate search strategy in a given information source or in multiple information sources.

Possible Measurement Techniques
- Annotated bibliography with search strategy discussion included
- Collaborative learning exercise in class
- Practical exercise practicum examination
- Research journal
- Research paper proposal
- Research portfolio
- Research worksheet

…will be able to discuss the importance of the intended audience in determining the appropriate information source.

Possible Measurement Techniques
- Annotated bibliography with search strategy discussion included
- Collaborative learning exercise in class
- Practical exercise
- Practicum examination
- Research journal
- Research paper proposal
- Research portfolio
- Research worksheet

…will be able to locate basic information in appropriate resources, and given a citation for an information source, will be able identify the elements needed to locate the information source.

Possible Measurement Techniques
- Research worksheet
- Short answer examination

…will be able to use access points (through key words, Boolean logic, proximity searching, truncation, and browsing) to identify useful information or information sources.

Possible Measurement Techniques

- Annotated bibliography with search strategy discussion included
- Collaborative learning exercise in class
- Practical exercise
- Practicum examination
- Research journal
- Research paper proposal
- Research portfolio
- Research worksheet

…after executing a search in an access tool, such as a periodical index or an online catalog, will be able to locate the identified item.

Possible Measurement Techniques

- Practical assignment
- Research portfolio
- Research worksheet
- Short answer examination

…after executing a search in a direct information source, such as a directory or full-text database, will be able to locate the desired information.

Possible Measurement Techniques

- Practical assignment
- Research portfolio
- Research worksheet
- Short answer examination

…will be able to evaluate information to determine its relevance, accuracy, and significance, and discuss how to select the best source for a given information problem.

Possible Measurement Techniques

- Annotated bibliography with search strategy discussion included
- Essay examination
- Research journal
- Research paper proposal
- Research portfolio

…given various information sources that might be appropriate for a specific information problem, will be able to discuss relevant characteristics that will help select the best source(s).

Possible Measurement Techniques

- Essay examination
- Research journal
- Research portfolio

…will know when to seek the advice of experts (including librarians) and how to ask for advice; be able to discuss in general when the limits of information seeking ability have been exhausted.

Possible Measurement Techniques

- Essay examination
- Pathfinder assignment
- Practical problem to solve
- Practicum examination that includes a "dead end"

…once realizing the need to consult an information expert, will be able to structure a question, summarize his or her search strategy, and report the information sources already consulted.

Possible Measurement Techniques

- Essay examination
- Pathfinder assignment
- Practical problem to solve
- Practicum examination that includes a "dead end"

…will know how to use information to solve a problem or answer a research question and will be able to synthesize the information found to document the thesis statement.

Possible Measurement Techniques

- Annotated bibliography
- Research paper
- Documented speech
- Research paper proposal

…will be able to select the most relevant information to solve an information problem.

Possible Measurement Techniques

- Annotated bibliography with information about the search strategy
- Documented speech
- Research paper

…will appreciate standards for the attribution of ideas, for handling quoted materials, and for the presentation of various perspectives, and will be able to discuss the role of attribution in the process of seeking information and reporting results.

Possible Measurement Techniques

- Essay examination

…will be able to use citations correctly in a paper that reports the results of an information problem.

Possible Measurement Techniques

- Annotated bibliography
- Documented speech
- Research paper
- Research paper proposal

From *An Educator's Guide to Information Literacy: What Every High School Senior Needs to Know*. Westport, CT: Libraries Unlimited, 2007. Copyright © 2007 by Ann Marlow Riedling.

…will be able to use citations to identify and locate sources of pertinent information.

Possible Measurement Techniques

- Annotated bibliography
- Documented speech
- Practical problem to solve
- Practicum examination
- Research paper
- Research paper proposal
- Research portfolio

Formative Assessments for Standard 2

The information literate student accesses needed information effectively and efficiently.

Assessment 2.1
(Teacher Assessment of Students)

Assign students to research a particular topic in the library. Grade their work based on these criteria: accuracy, completeness, choice of appropriate sources, variety of resources used, and so on. (You may assign each student a different topic or all may use the same topic.)

Ask students to browse the library stacks where the books in the discipline are shelved. Have students consult a volume of a relevant specialized encyclopedia and an index. Also, allow them to examine the contents of several journals in the discipline. Have your students write an essay in response to these questions:

- What is a (discipline)? In other words, how might it be defined?
- How might the resources consulted be utilized in other courses, especially in other disciplines?
- From this exercise, what have you learned about the scope of the discipline?
- Identify significant people in the discipline. Consult a variety of biographical resources and subject encyclopedias to gain a broader appreciation for the context in which important accomplishments were achieved.
- Identify a significant event or publication in the discipline. Try to ascertain the important people involved by consulting a variety of library resources.
- Contrast two journal articles or editorials from recent publications reflecting conservative and liberal tendencies. (It might be interesting to carry out this exercise again using publications from the late 1960s.)

Assign readings on a topic from both primary and secondary sources. Have students compare and contrast the sources and content.

Inherent in research is the critical evaluation of resources and their contents. The following assignments can help students develop the frequently overlooked skill of critical evaluation.

- Provide students with a popular and a scholarly article on the same topic. To encourage them to learn how to distinguish between these types of publications, have students analyze the articles using a prepared checklist of characteristics.
- Ask students to find a short article in the popular press and the original research finding on which the popular article was based. Students should review related findings, discuss the relationship between the popular article and original research, and critique the popular article with regard to its accuracy.
- Ask students to update a literature review done about five years ago on a topic in the discipline. They will have to utilize printed and electronic resources to identify pertinent information.

From *An Educator's Guide to Information Literacy: What Every High School Senior Needs to Know*. Westport, CT: Libraries Unlimited, 2007. Copyright © 2007 by Ann Marlow Riedling.

Assessment 2.2
(Student Self Assessment)

Checklist: Internet Basics and History

I use networks on a daily basis to access and communicate information. I can serve as
an active participant in a school or organizational planning group, giving advice and
providing information about networks. I can recommend several ways of obtaining
Internet access to others = 4

I can describe what a computer network does and how it can be useful personally and
professionally. I can distinguish between a local area network, a wide area network,
and the Internet and can describe educational uses for each. I can describe the history of
the Internet, recognize its international character, and know to a degree the extent of its
resources. I know the purpose and historical significance of newsgroups, gophers, and
telnet. I have personal access to the Internet that allows me to receive and send
e-mail, download files, and access the World Wide Web. I know that I must protect my
password, and should restrict access by others to my account = 3

I can identify some personal or professional uses for networks, and understand they may
have a value to my students and to me. I've read some articles about the Internet in the
popular press. I can directly use network access to a library catalog or CD-ROM = 2

I do not understand how networks work, nor can I identify any personal or professional uses
for networks, including the Internet. I do not have an account on any network nor would
I know how to get one = 1

Checklist: The World Wide Web

I can configure my Web browser with a variety of helper applications. I understand what
cookies do and whether to keep them enabled. I can speak to the security issues of
online commerce and data privacy = 4

I can use a Web browser like Explorer or Netscape to find information on the World Wide
Web, and can list some of the Web's unique features. I can explain the terms: hypertext,
URL, http, and html. I can write URLs to share information locations with others. I can
use Web search engines to locate subject specific information and can create bookmarks
to Web sites of educational value = 3

I am aware that the World Wide Web is a means of sharing information on the Internet.
I can browse the Web for recreational purposes = 2

I do not use the World Wide Web = 1

Checklist: Search Tools and Evaluation Strategies

I can identify some specialized search tools for finding software and e-mail addresses. I can speculate on future developments in online information searching and other kinds of intelligent search agents = 4

I can conduct an efficient search of Internet resources using directories like Yahoo or search engines like Google, Lycos, or Infoseek. I can use advanced search commands to specify and limit the number of hits I get. I can state some guidelines for evaluating the relevance of sites and the quality of the information I find on the Internet. I can write a bibliographic citation for information found = 3

I can occasionally locate useful information on the Internet by browsing or through remembered sources = 2

I cannot locate any information on the Internet = 1

Formative Assessments for Standard 3

The information literate student evaluates information and its sources critically and incorporates selected information into his or her knowledge base and value system.

Assessment 3.1
(Teacher Assessment of Students)

Advanced Information Literacy

As individuals move forward in their fields of study and specialization, their information needs change and the level of information literacy they need changes as well. In addition to the skills defined as basic information literacy, an individual who operates at the advanced level of information literacy:

...possesses sophisticated and in-depth knowledge of the literature of a particular discipline or field of study, how it is organized, and how it is transmitted, and can discuss the special characteristics of literature in a particular discipline or field of study, recognizing that individuals or groups identify themselves as belonging to specific areas and/or disciplines.

Possible Measurement Techniques

- Essay examination (for example, name five print resources that provide current information in your field of study; are there more print or electronic resources in your field of study, etc.)
- Pathfinder assignment (created by student). The goal of the pathfinder is for you to synthesize all the information you learn in the course into a single document. This document will represent a reference specialty, an area of expertise that you, as a reference librarian, could conceivably hold. The pathfinder should demonstrate the following: Audience, Sources, Pathfinder as a Genre.Research Journal.
- Research portfolio

...is able to discuss the ways in which individuals in these groups combine information from information sources with original thought, experimentation, and/or analysis to produce new information sources.

Possible Measurement Techniques

- Essay examination
- Pathfinder assignment (created by student)
- Research journal
- Research portfolio

...will recognize the major types of citations and know when they typically occur (documentary notes, in-text citations, bibliographic entries, etc.).

Possible Measurement Techniques

- Essay examination
- Pathfinder assignment
- Research journal

...will be able to discuss how scholars communicate in a discipline or field of study, identifying the most important channels of communication.

Possible Measurement Techniques

- Essay examination
- Pathfinder assignment
- Research journal

…knows the major information resources in a discipline and can identify specific important information sources in the discipline or field of study.

Possible Measurement Techniques

- Annotated bibliography
- Documented speech
- Practical problem to solve
- Practicum examination
- Research paper
- Research paper proposal
- Research portfolio

… will be able to complete a research assignment that uses the most important and relevant information sources for the information problem drawn from all available sources.

Possible Measurement Techniques

- Documented speech
- Research paper or thesis
- Research paper or thesis proposal

…evaluates the reliability and significance of information found in context of knowledge of the discipline and is able to identify the most reliable information sources for a given information problem.

Possible Measurement Techniques

- Annotated bibliography
- Essay examination
- Research portfolio

…will be able to discuss how the technology itself may shape the information carried.

Possible Measurement Techniques

- Essay examination
- Research journal
- Research portfolio

…will be able to discuss the economic and political forces which affect information.

Possible Measurement Techniques

- Essay examination
- Research journal
- Research portfolio

…understands how all of the skills of basic and advanced information literacy are used to support ideas and/or to create new knowledge, and develops a system to classify and handle the information located in research and to transfer information into a personal information system.

Possible Measurement Techniques

- Research paper
- Research portfolio

Formative Assessments for Standard 4

The information literate student, individually or as a member of a group, uses information effectively to accomplish a specific purpose.

Assessment 4.1
(Teacher Assessment of Students)

Students maintain a journal or diary of their research process. They record their thinking about the topic, questions they wish to answer, key words, and the progress of their research. For each resource consulted, the student discusses how it was searched, key words used and how well they worked, what was found, and any changes to the research topic.

Instructor Checklist

	Questions	Keywords	Progress	Changes
Student 1				
Student 2				
Student 3				

Assessment 4.2
(Teacher Assessment of Self)

Modification of Instructional Delivery

I continuously try new approaches suggested by research or observation to discover the most effective means of using technology to engage my students and meet curricular goals. I work with a team of fellow teachers to create, modify and improve my practices in this area = 4

I use a variety of instructional delivery methods and student grouping strategies routinely throughout the year. I can design activities and approaches that both best fit the learning objectives and the availability of the technology to me. I can use small groups working cooperatively or in rotation to take advantage of student-to-equipment ratios of greater than one-to-one = 3

I have tried units or projects that are student-directed, use small groups, or are highly individualized, but I primarily use teacher-directed, whole group instruction = 2

I have one or two effective methods of delivering content to my students. I do not use technology that requires that I change my instructional methodology = 1

Assessment 4.3
(Teacher Assessment of Students)

When gathering information, the team:

  Selects information with clear criteria in mind = 5
  Gathers and selects information purposefully = 4
  Shows ability to gather and select information = 3
  Is generally on track gathering information = 2
  Wanders off track and wastes time = 1

When organizing information, the team:

  Organizes information in a logically consistent and thoughtful manner = 5
  Organizes information in a logical manner = 4
  Is able to organize information = 3
  Shows some skill approaching the problem in a logical manner = 2
  Shows little skill approaching the problem in a logical manner = 1

When using information, the team:

  Shows high level of skill in drawing conclusions from information = 5
  Draws conclusions from information = 4
  Seems unclear about how to use information to reach a conclusion = 3
  Demonstrates some purpose for data gathering = 2
  Demonstrates little purpose for data gathering = 1

When thinking about information, the team:

  Clearly demonstrates divergent thinking and works toward insight level = 5
  Uses some divergent thinking in their approach = 4
  Shows little divergent thinking = 3
  Shows virtually no divergent thinking = 2
  Exhibits no creative or divergent thinking = 1

When organizing the information, the team:

  Organizes and presents its findings, conclusions, and recommendations convincingly = 5
  Presents its findings, conclusions, and recommendations in an organized manner = 4
  Presents findings, conclusions, and recommendations with some degree of organization = 3
  Is able to place information, findings, and graphics into the presentation template, but
    lacks organization = 2
  Is disorganized in its approach to making the presentation = 1

Persuasiveness

  Makes a dramatic and compelling argument = 5
  Makes a credible effort to persuade the audience = 4
  Shows some evidence of persuasion = 3
  Shows little evidence of persuasion = 2
  Is not at all persuasive in presentation = 1

Teamwork

  Works as a cohesive unit to make the presentation = 5
  Works as a group to make the presentation = 4
  Works together to make the presentation = 3
  Shows a limited ability to work together to make the presentation = 2
  Is unable to work together to make the presentation = 1

Audience Involvement

  Dramatically appeals to and engages their audience = 5
  Actively engages the audience in the presentation = 4
  Has little interaction with the audience = 3
  Has no interaction with the audience = 2
  Seems fearful or nervous, avoiding interaction with audience = 1

Effective Use of Technology

  Uses technology as a higher effective tool = 5
  Uses technology to enhance the message = 4
  Uses technology to some extent to demonstrate the group's position = 3
  Does not use technology in a persuasive manner = 2
  Shows lack of basic technology skills = 1

Formative Assessments for Standard 5

The information literate student understands many of the ethical, legal, and socio-economic issues surrounding the use of information and accesses and uses information ethically and legally.

Assessment 5.1
(Teacher Assessment of Self)

Ethical Use Understanding

I am aware of other controversial aspects of technology use including data privacy, equitable access, and free speech issues. I can speak to a variety of technology issues at my professional association meetings, to parent groups, and to the general community = 4

I clearly understand the difference between freeware, shareware, and commercial software and the fees involved in the use of each. I know the programs for which the district or my building holds a site license. I understand the school board policy on the use of copyrighted materials. I demonstrate ethical usage of all software and let my students know my personal stand on legal, moral, and safety issues involving technology. I know and enforce the school's technology policies and guidelines, including its Internet Acceptable Use Policy. I have a personal philosophy I can articulate regarding the use of technology in education = 3

I know that some copyright restrictions apply to computer software = 2

I am not aware of any ethical issues surrounding computer use = 1

Assessment 5.2
(Teacher Assessment of Self)

Netiquette, Online Ethics, and Current Issues Surrounding Internet Use

I can use my knowledge of the Internet to write good school policies and activities that help students develop good judgment and good information skills = 4

I have read a guideline for Internet use and follow the rules outlined. I know and read the FAQ files associated with sources on the Internet. I am aware that electronic communication is a new communication medium that may require new sensitivities. I can list some of the critical components of a good Acceptable Use Policy and know and use our district's policy = 3

I understand a few rules that my students and I should follow when using the Internet. I understand that the Internet is sometimes a controversial resource that many educators and parents do not understand = 2

I am not aware of any ethics or proprieties regarding the Internet nor am I aware of any issues dealing with Internet use in a school setting = 1

From *An Educator's Guide to Information Literacy: What Every High School Senior Needs to Know*. Westport, CT: Libraries Unlimited, 2007. Copyright © 2007 by Ann Marlow Riedling.

Assessment 5.3
(Teacher Assessment of Self)

Importance

Let the students know that the assignment has a specific understood purpose and communicate why learning how to find information is important to their success in class, in college, and throughout their careers. If they're not interested in scholarly research, point out that information exists on any topic, from buying a new stereo to planning a trip to Europe. If you have a personal story that illustrates the power of information, tell it.

Goals

Think about what you want the students to gain from the assignment. Just as you cannot teach a semester course in one day, information literacy cannot be achieved in one assignment. For anything other than a large research paper, consider focusing on a particular collection, research tool, or skill such as finding reference books on a topic, using a specific periodical database, or evaluating information.

Expectations

Don't assume students know how to use the library, even if they tell you they do. The majority of students have never been presented with the number of information choices they find in a university library. They also do not enter college understanding the organization of information within a discipline, how to search computerized databases, or how to evaluate information.

Relevancy

Try to tie information seeking into class assignments or to some area of student interest. Assignments asking students to find things for no particular reason (i.e., the scavenger or treasure hunt) are often considered busy work by the students, are actively resented, and have been proven to be ineffectual.

Reality

Don't ask your students to do something that can't be done. An impossible assignment frustrates a student and turns them against the library. Try doing the assignment yourself to test its feasibility and see if there are enough books and periodicals available in the library to sufficiently cover the assignment requirements. For additional help on determining the feasibility of an assignment as it relates to the library's collections and holdings, check with your subject librarian or contact Sarah Blakeslee at sblakeslee@csuchico.edu or Kris Johnson at kajohnson@csuchico.edu.

Clarity and Accuracy

Be specific in what you want the students to do and how you direct them to do it. If you want them to use scholarly articles, be sure they are clear on what distinguishes a scholarly journal from a popular journal. If you want students to look for articles in PsycInfo, don't tell them to go to a library computer and find it on the Internet. Instead direct them to the online database.

Topic

Choosing a topic is often difficult for students. Although everybody writing on the same topic creates difficulties in keeping material on the shelf, too wide a choice of topics paralyzes many students and often finds them researching inappropriate subjects for which they can find very little information. Consider offering your students a list of possible choices that you have pre-researched and know will result in a successful research experience. If it is necessary to have all the students write on one topic, or refer to one source, consider putting that item on reserve in a limited loan area.

Critical Thinking

Create an assignment that requires the student to think about the information they are retrieving such as comparing two sources or finding two viewpoints. Often students will take the first things they find on a topic, if not given a reason to be more discriminating.

Pace the Assignment

For large research assignments, break them into smaller chunks so you can ascertain whether or not the student is understanding the research process and finding the right sources. Looking at a draft bibliography can help you direct student research and also gives students enough time to use interlibrary loan if needed. Additionally, pacing the assignment discourages procrastination.

Internet

Explain to students the difference between public Web documents found through Web search engines and structured scholarly information databases such as ERIC or Medline available via the Web. Students are often told by instructors *not* to use the Internet for a class assignment when in reality the majority of our periodical databases are only accessible via the Internet.

Technology

Make sure students understand the technology required and have reasonable access to the computers and software necessary to complete assignments.

From *An Educator's Guide to Information Literacy: What Every High School Senior Needs to Know*. Westport, CT: Libraries Unlimited, 2007. Copyright © 2007 by Ann Marlow Riedling.

Assessment 5.4
(Teacher Assessment of Students)

Quiz

1. What are copyrighted materials?

2. What is an Acceptable Use Policy? Why do we need them?

3. Give five examples of proper online Netiquette.

4. How do you access an online periodical database?

5. What is the difference between using scholarly and popular magazines?

6. What is the difference between a search engine and a subject directory?

7. What is a draft?

6

Integrating Information Literacy Skills into the Curriculum

Collaboration is Key: Review of the Literature

According to Mackey and Jacobson, "Collaboration among faculty and librarians is essential for Information Literacy (IL) initiatives to be successful. These partnerships must be cultivated through ongoing planning, dialogue and classroom practice. IL is often viewed as a library concern in which librarians are responsible for program development and instruction, but this assumption must be changed to integrate the roles of faculty as full partners in a collaborative endeavor" (2005, p. 140).

Scott and O'Sullivan state, "Accomplishing [information literacy] requires co-operation, collaboration, and support between departments and the library, between teachers and [library media specialists], and a commitment from the administration to promote this atmosphere. Teachers at all levels of education...continue to struggle with exactly how to effectively integrate information literacy skills into their curriculum. The key is for teachers to analyze the content of their classes and assignments and then determine which information literacy skills should be applied where and when. Information literacy skills must be incorporated throughout all areas of a school's curriculum, not just in library orientation classes or in isolated skills presentations" (2005, p. 23). Dupois (1997) explains, "Unless [both teachers and] librarians educate users about finding information, users will continue to underutilize and misuse information" (p. 98). Jean Donham (2003) remarks, "High school and college librarians can only be effective in [teaching] information literacy [skills] when they work in collaboration with faculty...An information literacy program fails if there is not effective teaching...instruction must occur at the point of need in order for students to be motivated. In addition, there needs to be active involvement of the students..." (p. 200).

Incorporating information literacy across curricula, in all programs and services, and throughout the administrative life of a university, requires the collaborative efforts of faculty, librarians, and administrators. Through lectures and by leading discussions, faculties establish the context for learning. Faculty also inspire students to explore the unknown, offer guidance on how best to fulfill information needs, and monitor students' progress. Academic librarians coordinate the evaluation and selection of intellectual resources for programs and services; organize and maintain collections and many points of access to information; and provide instruction to students and faculty who seek information. Administrators create opportunities for collaboration and staff development among faculty, librarians, and other professionals who initiate information literacy programs, lead in planning and budgeting for those programs, and provide ongoing resources to sustain them.

The Boyer Commission Report, *Reinventing Undergraduate Education*, recommends strategies that require students to actively engage in framing a significant question or set of questions, the research or creative exploration to find answers, and the communications skills to convey the results. Courses structured in such a way create student-centered learning environments where inquiry is the norm, problem solving becomes the focus, and thinking critically is part of the process. Such learning environments require information literacy competencies (Boyer 1998).

Breivik (2005) remarks, "Today, most of the responsibility for developing information literacy skills is being placed squarely on the shoulders of higher education—both by calls for reform and from the business sector and by default, as feeder schools fail to develop them in their students…by and large, higher education reform reports since [Boyer] have failed to explicitly articulate the need for information literacy skills… Despite the interest of some accreditors and evidence of the need for information literacy skills in the workplace, however, few campuses have systematically addressed this need…It is time for both technology and information literacy skills to be accepted as a core competency to be acquired systematically through all levels of formal learning. The effort to develop them should begin in the K–12 system. Instead, students emerging from schools today are often far less prepared to do research than their predecessors" (pp. 20–22).

According to Jenson (2005), "Because most, if not all, of the research that students now do at the college level is conducted online, the context for that research has been lost. The library itself has disappeared from the process, at least from the students' perspective…Why do professors campus-wide complain about the quality of their students' end products while at the same time students express equal frustration that they can't find anything on topics that in fact are widely addressed in literature?…What I have come to discover, however, is that students have trouble producing good research because they have not been given the foundation necessary for doing so in a world where research of the available literature, traditionally conducted hands-on in an actual library, is now conducted almost exclusively by looking at a computer monitor. In fact, students can be taught effective research skills despite the complexity of the electronic indexes and databases now used to do such work…Whose responsibility is it?… As excellent as the library staff is, they can hardly be expected to shoulder the task alone. Nor is the answer to simply let them loose…" (pp. 107–109).

Gaining skills in information literacy multiplies the opportunities for students' self-directed learning, as they become engaged in using a wide variety of information sources to expand their knowledge, ask informed questions, and sharpen their critical thinking for still further self-directed learning. Achieving competency in information literacy requires an understanding that this cluster of abilities is not extraneous to the curriculum but is woven into the curriculum's content, structure, and sequence. This curricular integration also affords many possibilities for furthering the influence and impact of such student-centered teaching methods as problem-based learning, evidence-based learning, and inquiry learning. Guided by faculty and others in problem-based approaches, students reason about course content at a deeper level than is possible through the exclusive use of lectures and textbooks. To take fullest advantage of problem-based learning, students must often use thinking skills requiring them to become skilled users of information sources in many locations and formats, thereby increasing their responsibility for their own learning.

To obtain the information they seek for their investigations, students have many options. One is to utilize an information retrieval system, such as may be found in a library or in databases accessible by computer from any location. Another option is to select an appropriate investigative method for observing phenomena directly. For example, physicians, archaeologists, and astronomers frequently depend upon physical examination to detect the presence of particular phenomena. In addition, mathematicians, chemists, and physicists often utilize technologies such as statistical software or simulators to create artificial conditions in which to observe and analyze the interaction of phenomena. As students progress through K–12 schools, undergraduate years, and even graduate programs, they need to have repeated opportunities for seeking, evaluating, and managing information gathered from multiple sources and discipline-specific research methods.

Information Literacy Competency Standards for Higher Education (ACRL 2000) provides a framework for assessing the information literate individual. It also extends the work of the American Association of School Librarians Task Force on Information Literacy Standards, thereby providing higher education an opportunity to articulate its information literacy competencies with those of K–12 so that a continuum of expectations develops for students at all levels. The competencies presented in *Information Literacy Competency Standards for Higher Education* outline the process by which faculty; librarians and others pinpoint specific indicators that identify a student as information literate.

Students also find the competencies useful, because they provide them with a framework for gaining control over how they interact with information in their environment. It will help to sensitize them to the need to develop a metacognitive approach to learning, making them conscious of the explicit actions required for gathering, analyzing, and using information. All students are expected to demonstrate all of the competencies described in "x" document, but not everyone will demonstrate them to the same level of proficiency or at the same speed.

Furthermore, some disciplines may place greater emphasis on the mastery of competencies at certain points in the process, and therefore certain competencies would receive greater weight than others in any rubric for measurement. Many of the competencies are likely to be performed recursively, in that the reflective and evaluative aspects included within each standard will require the student to return to an earlier point in the process, revise the information seeking approach, and repeat the same steps.

To implement the standards fully, an institution should first review its mission and educational goals to determine how information literacy would improve learning and enhance the institution's effectiveness. To facilitate acceptance of the concept, faculty and staff development is also crucial.

One example of integration of information literacy skills into the curriculum is called The Libraries Information Literacy Curriculum (ILC). A coordinated approach to information literacy, integrated into the curricula of the schools and departments, will serve to prepare students with the ability to identify, locate, evaluate, and utilize information resources effectively throughout their lives. The ILC project is occurring at Purdue University and can be explored at the following Web site: www.lib.purdue.edu/rguides/instructionalservices/ilcgoals.html.

Collaboration between an instructor and a library media specialist leads to student achievement. According to a Colorado study, "A central finding of this study is the importance of a collaborative approach to information literacy. Test scores rise... as library media specialists and instructors work together" (Lance, Rodney, and Hamilton-Pennell 2000, p. 7). This Colorado study was conducted to see if having a strong library program made a difference in students' reading scores on the Colorado State Assessment tests. It showed that a strong library media center with a full-time library media specialist, support staff, and a strong computer network led to higher student achievement regardless of social and economic factors in a community (Hamilton-Pennell, Lance, Rodney, and Hainer 2000). Studies in nine other states produced similar findings. Many of the studies showed the importance of instructor and library media specialist collaboration.

Helen (2005) explains, "Information literacy is a process that cannot be taught out of context, and it is, therefore, important that instruction is integrated into the curriculum. Students require regular practice finding, evaluating, and using information. Collaboration means that better teaching and learning will occur because the [instructor] and [library media specialist] can support each other's strengths and accommodate each other's weaknesses. The [instructor] knows the subject content and the students' needs, while the [library media specialist] brings a host of other skills to the partnership" (p. 23).

An example of successful collaboration can be seen at the University at Albany, State University of New York. At Albany, "faculty and librarians work together on program planning, course development, course approval and teaching....Collaboration extends beyond the library and departments to include administration, teaching centers, and technology services... Librarians work with students on their research assignments, and are well informed about students' research skills and the resources available to them to complete their assignments. Librarians can therefore be a critical resource in the planning stages of a course... With the lines of communication open, faculty can provide input to librarians about student experiences with library resources, and offer suggestions for research materials, information organization in the library itself, technology access, databases, the library Web site, and tutorials. The work of faculty in the classroom can also provide librarians with essential feedback about the ways students interpret, analyze, and evaluate research materials within a disciplinary context... An exchange of ideas between faculty and librarians is always beneficial, but in many ways the synergy that happens through team teaching may offer students the best opportunity to apply information literacy within the context of a specific discipline" (Mackey and Jacobson 2005, p. 140). The Association of College & Research Libraries acknowledges a university's role in such learning: "Developing lifelong learners is central to the mission of higher education institutions. By ensuring that individuals have the intellectual abilities of reasoning and critical thinking, and by helping them construct a framework for learning how to learn, colleges and universities provide the foundation for continued growth throughout their careers, as well as in their roles as informed citizens and members of communities" (ACRL 2000, p. 4).

6.1: Teacher/Librarian: Collaborative Planning

Teacher(s) planning times:

Unit or Project: Library needed:

Essential question(s), goal(s), objective(s) *What do we want students to know and be able to do?*	Information literacy process *What part will we focus on?* ☐ **defines** problem or question ☐ **plans** effectively ☐ **locates** information ☐ **evaluates** information critically ☐ **extracts and records** relevant information ☐ **comprehends and organizes** information ☐ **synthesizes and communicates** creatively ☐ **cites** information sources ☐ **participates** effectively in groups ☐ **self-assesses** product and process Building Blocks of Research	Directions to student *What will we say and do to set the stage, define the purpose, and create interest?*
Learning activities *Teacher:* *Librarian:*	Ongoing assessments *How will we know if the student understands?* *Teacher:* *Librarian:*	Interim work checks: *Teacher:* *Librarian:*
Culminating task, product	Assessment *Teacher:* *Librarian:*	Student self-assessment
Resources needed (technology, materials, support, expertise)		

Permission granted by Debbie Abilock, 2006.

From *An Educator's Guide to Information Literacy: What Every High School Senior Needs to Know*. Westport, CT: Libraries Unlimited, 2007. Copyright © 2007 by Ann Marlow Riedling.

6.2: Information Literacy: An Overview of Design, Process, and Outcomes

The Building Blocks of Research

Information Literacy is a transformational process in which the learner needs to find, understand, evaluate, and use information in various forms to create for personal, social, or global purposes.

Information literacy shares a fundamental set of core thinking and problem-solving metaskills with other disciplines. Authentic cross-disciplinary problems that include observation and inference, analysis of symbols and models, comparison of perspectives, and assessment of the rhetorical context engage students in developing mastery of information literacy over time.

Information Literacy	Student Skills and Strategies	Student Outcomes	Curriculum and Teaching Design
A problem-solving process for: • exploring and questioning • defining an information need • creating a plan to locate relevant information • reading the medium • synthesizing information to create knowledge • applying insight to personal, social, or global contexts to create wisdom • self-evaluating the process and the product	The student uses habits of mind: • recognize problems • formulate hypotheses • make good predictions • ask important questions • locate, analyze, interpret, evaluate, and record information and ideas • assume multiple stances • apply heuristic strategies • develop complex understanding • extend understanding through creative models • apply understanding to new problems	The student is a learner: • independent • disciplined • planful • self-motivated • metacognitive • flexible • adventurous	The learning design provides: • authentic contexts • simulations, real applications, and problems • reiterative opportunities for unique performances • ongoing assessments • longitudinal rubrics • integration of information literacy • creative roles for teachers • collegiality • culture of innovation

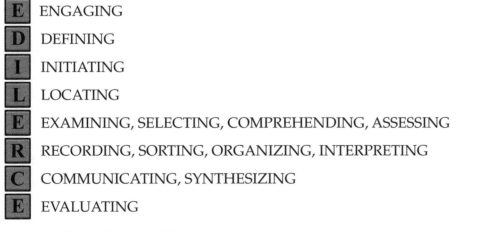

E ENGAGING

D DEFINING

I INITIATING

L LOCATING

E EXAMINING, SELECTING, COMPREHENDING, ASSESSING

R RECORDING, SORTING, ORGANIZING, INTERPRETING

C COMMUNICATING, SYNTHESIZING

E EVALUATING

Permission granted by Debbie Abilock, 2006.

From *An Educator's Guide to Information Literacy: What Every High School Senior Needs to Know*. Westport, CT: Libraries Unlimited, 2007. Copyright © 2007 by Ann Marlow Riedling.

6.3: Leveraging Tools: Inventory the Opportunity

Effective teaching with technology matches the teacher's goals and the learner's characteristics and needs with tools that enhance understanding.

TEACHING PARTNER	LEARNERS	SELF-ASSESSMENT	TOOL
How does this person teach? (level of control, beliefs about learners) Collaboration track record?	What are your learners' characteristics? (needs, interests, strengths)	How do you teach? (level of control, beliefs about learners)	Baskets Definitions Screenings Scripts Packages Structured Communities Communities of Practice Inquiry
Are there "ingredients" that are always included? Are there problems that the teacher sees every year?	What "ingredients" do the students always like? Where do the students always seem "in trouble"?	What "ingredients" do you like to include? What problems do you encounter or see every year?	Baskets Definitions Screenings Scripts Packages Structured Communities Communities of Practice Inquiry
How does this teacher think about change? What is nonnegotiable?	Will the kids have input? Give feedback?	What flexibility will be asked of you? What is nonnegotiable?	Baskets Definitions Screenings Scripts Packages Structured Communities Communities of Practice Inquiry
How much time is available for meeting?	How much time is planned for student learning?	How much time do you have available?	Baskets Definitions Screenings Scripts Packages Structured Communities Communities of Practice Inquiry
How much computing is available?	Do the students have good access to computers at home? Comfort with technology?	What technology expertise do you need to have?	Baskets Definitions Screenings Scripts Packages Structured Communities Communities of Practice Inquiry
What are the goals of the project? What are the goals for the learners?	What do students learn?	What are the goals of the project? What are the goals for the learners?	Baskets Definitions Screenings Scripts Packages Structured Communities Communities of Practice Inquiry

From *An Educator's Guide to Information Literacy: What Every High School Senior Needs to Know.* Westport, CT: Libraries Unlimited, 2007. Copyright © 2007 by Ann Marlow Riedling.

6.4: Mapping Information Literacy: A Problem-Solving Process

Grade 1	Grade 2	Grade 3	Grade 4	Grade 5	Grade 6	Grade 7	Grade 8	Grade 9	Grade 10	Grade 11	Grade 12
Understanding the context											
Browsing and grazing											
Defining a need Stating a goal Forming a focus Asking a question											
Identifying Likely sources Designing a search strategy											
Locating resources											
Assessing suitability to task Identifying missing information											
Revising search strategy											
Comprehending											
Recording information											
Organizing information											
Interpreting information Comparing, judging, analyzing											
Synthesizing a position Developing a point of view Forming a conclusion											
Communicating the information											
Self-evaluating process											
Self-evaluating product											

Permission granted by Debbie Abilock, 2006.

From *An Educator's Guide to Information Literacy: What Every High School Senior Needs to Know*. Westport, CT: Libraries Unlimited, 2007. Copyright © 2007 by Ann Marlow Riedling.

6.5: Information Literacy Essential Questions

Grade 1	Grade 2	Grade 3	Grade 4	Grade 5	Grade 6	Grade 7	Grade 8	Grade 9	Grade 10	Grade 11	Grade 12
Understanding the context	Why does context matter? How much do I need to know before I understand?										
Browsing and grazing grazing	How do I choose what to examine and what to ignore?										
Defining a need, stating a goal, forming a focus, asking a question	What is the information problem I am trying to solve? What do I need to know? What are the characteristics of a focus? What is the purpose of a question?										
Identifying likely sources, designing a search strategy	Why plan before I search? Why are some sources more likely to be useful for this need? What would the very best results look like? How is a strategy different than a rule?										
Locating resources	How is my access to information affected by its arrangement or organization?										
Assessing suitability to task, identifying missing information	How do I determine what is appropriate to my need? What are my "blind spots" in searching? Why are some "voices" missing?										
Revising search strategy	How do I know when to stop searching?										
Comprehending the information	How do I know I understand what I am reading? What do I do when I don't understand the information?										
Recording information	What is the value of attributing the ideas and words of others?										

(Continued)

From *An Educator's Guide to Information Literacy: What Every High School Senior Needs to Know.* Westport, CT: Libraries Unlimited, 2007. Copyright © 2007 by Ann Marlow Riedling.

Information Literacy Essential Questions (*Continued*)

Grade 1	Grade 2	Grade 3	Grade 4	Grade 5	Grade 6	Grade 7	Grade 8	Grade 9	Grade 10	Grade 11	Grade 12
Interpreting information, comparing, judging, analyzing	How can I explain contradictions? From whose perspective is this information, and how does that affect my evaluation? What is valid evidence?										
Synthesizing a position, developing a point of view, forming a conclusion	What common misconceptions might my audience have? What biases and assumptions do I have? Can I imagine variables – what if...? What part of my position or conclusion is a theory? opinion? fact? How does this relate to me? So what – why does this matter?										
Communicating the information	How are my views about this shaped by the form of communication I use?										
Self-evaluating process	What are my strengths and weaknesses in information literacy? What do I do when I don'I know what to do? How is an information literate person like a poet? like a scientist?										
Self-evaluating product	How can I best show this information? What does my audience fail to learn from this format?										

Permission granted by Debbie Abilock, 2006.

From *An Educator's Guide to Information Literacy: What Every High School Senior Needs to Know*. Westport, CT: Libraries Unlimited, 2007. Copyright © 2007 by Ann Marlow Riedling.

6.6: A Context for Collaboration

Assessment

What does assessment look like?

1. *What is assessment?*
2. How are *alternative* products, performances, and processes assessed?
3. What kinds of *feedback* help students learn?
4. How can *lesson study* assess students as they work? What is the lesson study *cycle*?
5. How can we assess student work *collaboratively*?
6. What is the process for designing *performance assessment tasks*?
7. What design principles are essential in *rubric construction*? Creators: *Rubistar, Scoring Guide for Student Products, Teachnology Rubrics*; Teacher-created example: Socratic Seminar; Student-created examples: #1 #2
8. What are *portfolio assessments*? *anthology portfolios*? *digital portfolios*?
9. How does a *scoring guide* assess student technology products? *example*
10. What other assessment guides can help us? *6+1 writing, reading,* and *oral communication*
11. Can I *retool quizzes* to test higher level thinking?
12. What's the *difference* between thinking maps and organizers? (*examples*)
13. How can we help students assess their own learning? (examples #1, #2 , #3)
14. Capture mouse and audio of student online using *Camtasia Studio* (Moyo usability studies at Penn State).
15. How will we *gather feedback from students* on our teaching?
16. How we *measure our own current practices* against a set of indicators for engaged learning and high performance technology?

Effective teaching matches the teacher's goals and the learner's characteristics and needs with tools and methods that enhance understanding.

Permission granted by Debbie Abilock, 2006.

Conclusion

According to Bill Gates (2005), "When we looked at the millions of students that our high schools are not preparing for higher education—and we looked at the damaging impact that has on their lives—we came to a painful conclusion: America's high schools are obsolete. By obsolete, I don't just mean that our high schools are broken, flawed, and under-funded—though a case could be made for every one of those points. By obsolete, I mean that our high schools—even when they're working exactly as designed—cannot teach our kids what they need to know today. Training the workforce of tomorrow with the high schools of today is like trying to teach kids about today's computers on a 50-year-old mainframe. It's the wrong tool for the times. Our high schools were designed fifty years ago to meet the needs of another age. Until we design them to meet the needs of the 21st century, we will keep limiting—even ruining—the lives of millions of Americans every year. Today, only one-third of our students graduate from high school ready for college, work, and citizenship" (p. 2).

References

Abilock, D. 2004. Information literacy from prehistory to K–20: A new definition. *Knowledge Quest* 32(4):9–11.

Achieve, Inc. (2005). *Rising to the Challenge. Are High School Graduates Prepared for College and Work?* http://www.achieve.org (accessed May 4, 2006).

American Library Association and Association for Educational Communications and Technology (ALA & AECT). 1998. *Information power: Building partnerships for learning.* Chicago: American Library Association.

Association of College & Research Libraries (ACRL). 2000. *Information Literacy Competency Standards for Higher Education: Standards, Performance Indicators and Outcomes.* http://www.ala.org/ala/acrl/acrlstandards/informationliteracycompetency.htm (assessed January 3, 2005).

Bleakley, A., and J. C. Carrigan. 1994. *Resource-based learning activities.* Chicago: American Library Association.

Boekhorst, A. K., and J. J. Britz. 2004. Information literacy at school level: A comparative study between the Netherlands and South Africa. *Journal of Library and Information Science* 70(2):63–71.

Boyer, E. 1998. Commission Report: Reinventing Undergraduate Education.

Breivik, P. S. 1998. *Student learning in the information age.* Phoenix: Oryx Press.

Breivik, P. S. 2005. 21st century learning and information literacy. *Teacher Librarian* 37(2):20–28.

Conley, D. 2005. *Standards for Success. College Knowledge: What It Really Takes for Students to Succeed and What We Can Do to Get Them Ready.* San Francisco: Jossey-Bass.

Davis, E. 2004. Leveraging our cutting-edge library tools and resources—An information literacy success story. *Multimedia & Internet @ Schools* 11(5):25–27.

Deucker, P. 1992. Be Data Literate: Know What To Do.

Donham, J. 2003. My senior is your first year student. *Knowledge Quest,* 32(1).

Dorsaj, A. and I. Jukes. 2004. Understanding digital kids. *Teaching and Learning in the New Digital Landscape.* http://www.thecommittedsardine.net/infosavvy/education/handouts/handoutsmain.asp (accessed February 13, 2004).

Doyle, C. 1995. Information literacy in an information society. *Emergency Librarian* 72(4):30–35.

Dumont, A., and T. Fenoulhet. 1977. Towards a policy framework for the knowledge-based economy. In *Economics of the Information Society,* ed. A. Dumont and J. Dryden. Luxembourg: European Commission.

Dupois, E. 1997. The information literacy challenge: Addressing the changing needs of our students through our programs. In *The challenge of Internet literacy: The instruction-web convergence,* ed. Lyn Elizabeth M. Martin, 98. New York: Haworth Press.

Evans, J., and S. Harrar. 2002. Five habits of curious people. *Prevention* 55(38):31–37.

Gates, B. 2005. Prepared remarks, National Education Summit on High Schools.

Geck, C. 2006. The generation X connection: Teaching information literacy to the newest net generation. *Teacher Librarian* 33(3):19–23.

Gratch-Lindauer, B. 2004. Information literacy student behaviors. *College and Research Libraries News* 66(10):715–718.

Hamilton-Pennell, C., K. C. Lance, M. J. Rodney, and E. Hainer. 2000. Dick and Jane go to the head of the class. *School Library Journal* 46(4):44–47.

Haycock, K. 2006. Information literacy programs can foster disciplined inquiry. *Teacher Librarian* 33(3):38.

Heil, D. 2005. The internet and student research: Teaching critical evaluation skills. *Teacher Librarian* 33(2):26–29.

Helen, J. 2005. Help students and teachers become information literate. *Teacher Librarian* 32(5):22–24.

Hensley, R. B. 2004. Curiosity and creativity as attributes of information literacy. *Information Literacy and Instruction* 44(1):31–36.

Hoctor, M. 2005. Accessing information: The internet—a highway or a maze? *Gifted Child Today* 28(3):32–37.

Ishizuka, K. 2005. Internet users overly confident, but naïve. *School Library Journal* 51(3):19–19.

Jenson, J. 2004. It's the information age, so where is the information? *College Teaching* 52(3):107–112.

Kuhlthau, C. 1995. The instructional role of the library media specialist in the information age school. *Information for a new age.* Englewood, CO: Libraries Unlimited.

Lance, K. C., M. J. Rodney, and C. Hamilton-Pennell. 2000. *How school librarians help kids achieve standards: The second Colorado study.* San Jose, CA: Hi Willow Research and Publishing.

Levine, P. 2005. The problem of online misinformation and the role of schools. *Simile* 5(1).

Lou, Y., and K. MacGregor. 2004. Learning with internet resources: Task structure and group collaboration. Paper presented at the 12th International Conference of Society for Information Technology and Teacher Education, Orlando, FL.

McPherson, K. 2005. Online information literacy: Moving from the familiar to the new. *Teacher Librarian* 33(1):69–70.

Mackey, T. P., and T. E. Jacobson. 2005. Information literacy: A collaborative endeavor. *College Teaching* 54(4):140–144.

Mackey, T. P., and T. E. Jacobson. 2004. Integrating information literacy in lower and upper level courses: Developing sealable models for higher education. *The Journal of General Education* 53(3–4):201–224.

Miller, K. 2003. Novice teachers' perceptions of the role of the teacher-librarian in information literacy. *Canadian Association for School Libraries* 27(1).

Mittermeyer, D. 2005. Incoming first year undergraduate students: How information literate are they? *Education for Information* 23:203–232.

Moore, P. 2000. Primary school children's interaction with library media. *Teacher Librarian* 27(3):7–11.

Quarton, B. 2003. Research skills and the new undergraduate. *Journal of Instructional Psychology* 30(2):120–125.

Rockman, I. F. 2002. Strengthening connections between information literacy, general education and assessment efforts. *Library Trends* 51(2):185–198.

Rockman, I. F., and G. W. Smith. 2005. Information and communication technology literacy. *College & Research Libraries News* 66(8):587–589.

Rosen, J., and G. M. Castro. 2002. From workbook to web: Building an information literacy oasis. *Computers in Libraries* 22(1):30–36.

Scott, T. J., and M. K. O'Sullivan. 2005. Analyzing student search strategies: Making a case for integrating information literacy skills into the curriculum. *Teacher Librarian* 33(1):21–25.

Sellen, M. 2002. Information literacy in general education: A new requirement for the 21st century. *Journal of General Education* 51(2):115–126.

Todd, R. 2001. Transitions for preferred futures of school libraries: Knowledge space, not information place, connectors, not collections, actions, not positions, evidence, not advocacy. Keynote paper at the Virtual Conference Session, International Association of School Librarians. http://www.iasl-slo.org/virtualpaper2001.html (accessed August, 2006).

Whelan, D. 2003. Why isn't information literacy catching on? *School Library Journal.* http://www.schoollibraryjournal.com/article/CA318993 (accessed May 3, 2004).

Wilder, S. 2005. Information literacy makes all the wrong assumptions. *Chronicle of Higher Education* 51(18):B13.

Index

About the Author

ANN MARLOW RIEDLING has worked in the field of library science and information technology since 1974. Her previous books for Libraries Unlimited include *Helping Teachers Teach: A School Library Media Specialist's Role, 3rd Edition* and *Information Literacy: What Does it Look Like in the School Library Media Center*. She has written several other books in the school library fieldand a trade book entitled, *How We Became Camels*.